TEACHER'S PET PUBLICATIONS

LITPLAN TEACHER PACK
for

Scorpions
based on the book by
Walter Dean Myers

Written by
Barbara M. Linde, MA Ed.

© 1998 Teacher's Pet Publications
All Rights Reserved

This **LitPlan** for *Scorpions*
has been brought to you by Teacher's Pet Publications, Inc.

Copyright Teacher's Pet Publications 1998
11504 Hammock Point
Berlin MD 21811

Only the student materials in this unit plan (such as worksheets,
study questions, and tests) may be reproduced multiple times
for use in the purchaser's classroom.

For any additional copyright questions,
contact Teacher's Pet Publications.

www.tpet.com

TABLE OF CONTENTS *Scorpions*

Introduction	5
Unit Objectives	8
Reading Assignment Sheet	9
Unit Outline	10
Study Questions	13
Multiple Choice Quiz/Study Questions	20
Pre-Reading Vocabulary Worksheets	33
Lesson One (Introductory Lesson)	45
Writing Assignment 1	49
Oral Reading Evaluation Form	56
Writing Assignment 2	60
Writing Evaluation Form	61
Writing Assignment 3/Nonfiction Assignment	69
Nonfiction Assignment Sheet	70
Extra Writing Assignments/Discussion ?s	71
Project Ideas	74
Vocabulary Review Activities	77
Unit Review Activities	79
Unit Tests	85
Unit Resource Materials	115
Vocabulary Resource Materials	129

A FEW NOTES ABOUT THE AUTHOR
WALTER DEAN MYERS

MYERS, WALTER DEAN , 1937- Born Walter Milton Myers, in Martinsburg, West Virginia, his mother died when he was three. He was then adopted and raised by Florence and Herbert Dean. The Deans moved to Harlem shortly after. In *Something About the Author*, Volume 71, Myers said he "lived in an exciting corner of the renowned Black capital and in an exciting era. The people I met there, the things I did, have left a permanent impression on me."

Myers began reading at age four, and started writing when he was ten. Since his parents did not consider writing as a career possibility, he was not encouraged to write. He enlisted in the U. S. Army when he was seventeen, and served for three years. During that time he continued to read and write for pleasure. He attended City College of the City University of New York, and received a B. A. degree from Empire State College in 1984.

Winning a writing contest sponsored by the Council on Interracial Books for Children in the late 1960's changed his life. The winning entry, a picture book titled *Where Did the Day Go?*, was published in 1969. Myers continued writing after that. Most of his books center on Black teens growing up in an urban environment. In addition, Myers has written science fiction, non-fiction, mysteries, and adventure stories.

Awards include the ALA notable book citation in 1975 for *Fast Sam, Cool Clyde, and Stuff*, 1978 for *It Ain't All For Nothin'*, 1979 for *The Young Landlords*, and 1988 for *Me, Mop, and the Moondance Kid* and *Scorpions*. He also received several ALA Best Books for Young Adults citations, including 1988 for *Scorpions* and *Fallen Angels*. He received the Coretta Scott King Award for fiction in 1980 for *The Young Landlords*, in 1985 for *Motown and Didi*, and 1988 for *Fallen Angels*. *Scorpions* was a Newbery Honor Book in 1989. His most recent book, *Slam!*, has won the Coretta Scott King Award, and was named the ALA Best Book for Young Adults . Myers continues to live and write from his home in New Jersey.

Published Works

Where Does the Day Go? 1969
The Dragon Takes a Wife, 1972
The Dancers, 1972.
Fly, Jimmy, Fly!, 1974
Fast Sam, Cool Clyde, and Stuff, 1975
Brainstorm, 1977
Mojo and the Russians, 1977
Victory for Jamie, 1977
It Ain't All for Nothin', 1978
The Young Landlords, 1979
The Golden Serpent, 1980
The Black Pearl and the Ghost, 1980
Hoops, 1981
The Legend of Tarik, 1981
Won't Know Till I Get There, 1982

The Nicholas Factor, 1983
Tales of a Dead King, 1983
Motown and Didi: A Love Story, 1984
The Outside Shot, 1984
Sweet Illusions, 1986
Crystal, 1987
Scorpions, 1988
Me, Mop, and the Moondance Kid, 1988
Fallen Angels, 1988
The Mouse Rap, 1990
Somewhere in the Darkness, 1992
Mop, Moondance, and the Nagasaki Knights, 1992
The Righteous Revenge of Artemis Bonner, 1992
Slam! 1996

INTRODUCTION

This unit has been designed to develop students' reading, writing, thinking, listening and speaking skills through exercises and activities related to *Scorpions* by Walter Dean Myers. It includes twenty lessons, supported by extra resource materials.

The **introductory lesson** introduces students to one main theme of the novel, obstacles presented by living in an inner-city environment, through a bulletin board activity. Following the introductory activity, students are given an explanation of how the activity relates to the book they are about to read.

The **reading assignments** are approximately thirty pages each; some are a little shorter while others are a little longer. Students have approximately 15 minutes of pre-reading work to do prior to each reading assignment. This pre-reading work involves reviewing the study questions for the assignment and doing some vocabulary work for 8 to 10 vocabulary words they will encounter in their reading.

The **study guide questions** are fact-based questions; students can find the answers to these questions right in the text. These questions come in two formats: short answer or multiple choice. The best use of these materials is probably to use the short answer version of the questions as study guides for students (since answers will be more complete), and to use the multiple choice version for occasional quizzes. It might be a good idea to make transparencies of your answer keys for the overhead projector.

The **vocabulary work** is intended to enrich students' vocabularies as well as to aid in the students' understanding of the book. Prior to each reading assignment, students will complete a two-part worksheet for approximately 8 to 10 vocabulary words in the upcoming reading assignment. Part I focuses on students' use of general knowledge and contextual clues by giving the sentence in which the word appears in the text. Students are then to write down what they think the words mean based on the words' usage. Part II gives students dictionary definitions of the words and has them match the words to the correct definitions based on the words' contextual usage. Students should then have an understanding of the words when they meet them in the text.

After each reading assignment, students will go back and formulate answers for the study guide questions. Discussion of these questions serves as a **review** of the most important events and ideas presented in the reading assignments.

After students complete extra discussion questions, there is a **vocabulary review** lesson which pulls together all of the separate vocabulary lists for the reading assignments and gives students a review of all of the words they have studied.

Following the reading of the book, two lessons are devoted to the **extra discussion questions/writing assignments**. These questions focus on interpretation, critical analysis and personal response, employing a variety of thinking skills and adding to the students' understanding of the novel. These questions are done as a **group activity**. Using the information they have acquired so far through individual work and class discussions, students get together to further examine the text and to brainstorm ideas relating to the themes of the novel.

The group activity is followed by a **reports and discussion** session in which the groups share their ideas about the book with the entire class; thus, the entire class gets exposed to many different ideas regarding the themes and events of the book.

There are three **writing assignments** in this unit, each with the purpose of informing, persuading, or having students express personal opinions. The first assignment is to express a personal **opinion**: students will complete written and illustrated journal entries to respond to each chapter. The second assignment is to **persuade**: students will write a letter to Jamal to persuade him to get rid of the gun. The third assignment is to inform: students will write a report about a topic related to the themes or setting of the novel.

The **nonfiction reading assignment** for this unit will be done in conjunction with Writing Assignment #3. Students are required to read a piece of nonfiction related in some way to *Scorpions*. After reading their nonfiction pieces, students will fill out a worksheet on which they answer questions regarding facts, interpretation, criticism, and personal opinions. During one class period, students make **oral presentations** about the nonfiction pieces they have read. This not only exposes all students to a wealth of information, it also gives students the opportunity to practice **public speaking**.

The **review lesson** pulls together all of the aspects of the unit. The teacher is given four or five choices of activities or games to use which all serve the same basic function of reviewing all of the information presented in the unit.

The **unit test** comes in two formats: all multiple choice-matching-true/false or with a mixture of matching, short answer, and composition. As a convenience, two different tests for each format have been included.

There are additional **support materials** included with this unit. The **unit resource section** includes suggestions for an in-class library, crossword and word search puzzles related to the novel, and extra vocabulary worksheets. There is a list of **bulletin board ideas** which gives the teacher suggestions for bulletin boards to go along with this unit. In addition, there is a list of **extra class activities** the teacher could choose from to enhance the unit or as a substitution for an exercise the teacher might feel is inappropriate for his/her class. **Answer keys** are located directly after the **reproducible student materials** throughout the unit. The student materials may be reproduced for use in the teacher's classroom without infringement of copyrights. No other portion of this unit may be reproduced without the written consent of Teacher's Pet Publications, Inc.

UNIT PLAN ADAPTATIONS

Block Schedule

Depending on the length of your class periods, and the frequency with which the class meets, you may wish to choose one of the following options:
- Complete two of the daily lessons in one class period.
- Have students complete all reading and writing activities in class.
- Assign all reading to be completed out of class, and concentrate on the worksheets and discussions in class.
- Assign the projects from Daily Lesson Fifteen at the beginning of the unit, and allow time each day for students to work on them.
- Use some of the Unit and Vocabulary Resource activities during every class.

Gifted & Talented / Advanced Classes
- Emphasize the projects and the extra discussion questions.
- Have students complete all of the writing activities.
- Assign the reading to be completed out of class and focus on the discussions in class.
- Encourage students to develop their own questions.

ESL / ELD
- Assign a partner to help the student read the text aloud.
- Tape record the text and have the student listen and follow along in the text.
- Give the student the study guide worksheets to use as they read.
- Provide pictures and demonstrations to explain difficult vocabulary words and concepts.

UNIT OBJECTIVES *Scorpions*

1. Through reading *Scorpions,* students will analyze characters and their situations to better understand the themes of the novel.

2. Students will demonstrate their understanding of the text on four levels: factual, interpretive, critical, and personal.

3. Students will practice reading aloud and silently to improve their skills in each area.

4. Students will enrich their vocabularies and improve their understanding of the novel through the vocabulary lessons prepared for use in conjunction with it.

5. Students will answer questions to demonstrate their knowledge and understanding of the main events and characters in *Scorpions*.

6. Students will practice writing through a variety of writing assignments.

7. The writing assignments in this are geared to several purposes:

    a. To check the students' reading comprehension
    b. To make students think about the ideas presented by the novel
    c. To make students put those ideas into perspective
    d. To encourage critical and logical thinking
    e. To provide the opportunity to practice good grammar and improve students' use of the English language.

8. Students will read aloud, report, and participate in large and small group discussions to improve their public speaking and personal interaction skills.

UNIT OUTLINE - *Scorpions*

1 Introduction PVR 1-3	2 ??s 1-3 Writing Assignment 1 Journal Writing	3 PVR 4-5 Minilesson: Conflict	4 ??s 4-5 PVR 6-7 Minilesson: Dialect	5 ??s 6-7 PVR 8-9 Oral Reading Evaluation
6 ??s 8-9 Minilesson: Figurative Language	7 Quiz 1-9 PVR 10-12	8 Writing Assignment 2 Persuade	9 ??s 10-12 PVR 13-15	10 ??s 13-15 PVR 16-17 Minilesson: Character Traits
11 ??s 16-17 PVR 18-20 Writing Conferences	12 ??s 18-20 Minilesson: Story Map	13 Writing Assignment 3 Inform	14 Extra Discussion ??s	15 Cooperative Group Projects
16 Library Work	17 Vocabulary Review	18 Unit Review	19 Test	20 Non-fiction Presentations

Key: P = Preview Study Questions V = Prereading Vocabulary Worksheet R = Read

READING ASSIGNMENT LOG - *Scorpions*

Date Assigned	Chapters Assigned	Completion Date
	1-3	
	4-5	
	6-7	
	8-9	
	10-12	
	13-15	
	16-17	
	18-20	

WRITING ASSIGNMENT LOG - *Scorpions*

Date Assigned	Assignment	Completion Date
	Writing Assignment 1	
	Writing Assignment 2	
	Writing Assignment 3 Non-fiction Assignment	
	Project	

STUDY QUESTIONS

SHORT ANSWER STUDY QUESTIONS *Scorpions*

Chapters 1-3
1. Identify the main character and the members of his family.
2. What did Randy ask Mama for, and why?
3. What did Randy want Jamal to do? How did Mama feel about?
4. How did Jamal feel about Mack?
5. What did Jamal do well?
6. Describe the discussion between Jamal and Dwayne.
7. What were some of the things that made Jamal feel small inside?

Chapters 4-5
1. Who is Tito? What did he start to do right after he met Jamal?
2. Did Jamal want to talk to Mack? Why or why not?
3. How did Jamal feel about Randy? Why?
4. What did Mack tell Jamal about Randy?
5. Why didn't the Scorpions want Randy out of jail?
6. How did Mack suggest that Jamal get the money for Randy?
7. How old is Jamal?
8. What did Jamal think Randy was doing to Mama?

Chapters 6-7
1. Where did the boys go? What did they talk about?
2. What disease/illness did Tito have? How did Jamal react to it?
3. What did Jamal do when he got home after the fight with Dwayne?
4. What was Tito's reason for wanting to join the Scorpions?
5. What did Mack give to Jamal?

Chapters 8-9
1. How did Indian feel about having Jamal as the leader of the Scorpions?
2. What did Angel say about Jamal leading the Scorpions?
3. How did Jamal feel about Randy? About his father?
4. How did Jamal feel about the Scorpions?
5. How did Jamal feel when his father left? Why?
6. Jamal thought something Dwayne did was not right. What was it?

Chapters 10-12
1. Describe the fight between Jamal and Dwayne
2. What was Jamal doing as he went down the stairs?
3. Where did Tito and Jamal go when they left school? What did they do?
4. Describe the meeting between Jamal and Dwayne.
5. What kind of job did Jamal get?
6. Why was Tito crying?
7. What did Tito tell Abuela about the gun?
8. What did Jamal tell himself he should do with the gun? Did he think he would do it?

Short Answer Study Questions *Scorpions*

Chapters 13-15

1. Describe the meeting with Jamal, Mr. Davidson, Dwayne, and Mrs. Parsons.
2. Why did Mr. Davidson want to talk to Mrs. Hicks?
3. Where did Jamal go after the meeting?
4. What happened when Jamal got to Mr. Gonzalez's store?
5. What happened to Randy?
6. How did Sassy find out about the gun? Did she tell Mama about it?
7. What kind of sound did Mama make after she got home ?
8. Why didn't the Scorpions want Mack working with them?
9. Describe Indian's plan, and Mack's ideas.
10. What was Jamal's decision about the gun?

Chapters 16-17

1. Jamal made a phone call to Indian. What did he say? What was the reply?
2. What message did Angel give when he called back?
3. What was Jamal tell Tito he would do when he met Indian?
4. What did Mrs. Roberts want Jamal to do? Did he do it? Why or why not?
5. Did Dwayne and Jamal fight?
6. What did Mama ask Mr. Stanton? What was his reply?
7. What happened when Jamal and Tito met Indian and Angel in the park?

Chapters 18-20

1. What did the boys do with the gun?
2. What did Tito say was going to happen to him?
3. Jamal told Tito he could not come over for a week, because his mother was too upset about Randy. What was the real reason?
4. Where did Jamal and his family live?
5. What did Mack tell Jamal?
6. What happened to Tito?
7. What did Jamal give Tito?

ANSWER KEY: SHORT ANSWER STUDY QUESTIONS *Scorpions*

Chapters 1-3

1. Identify the main character and the members of his family.
    Jamal Hicks is a seventh grade boy. He lives with his younger sister, Sassy, who is in the third grade, and his mother. Randy is Jamal's seventeen year old brother. He is in prison for shooting someone.

2. What did Randy ask Mama for, and why?
    He wanted five hundred dollars so the lawyer could appeal his case.

3. What did Randy want Jamal to do? How did Mama feel about?
    Randy wanted Jamal to go and see Mack. Mama did not want Jamal to go near Mack or the other Scorpions.

4. How did Jamal feel about Mack?

    Jamal didn't like Mack. He was different, rather strange. Mack had already been in a juvenile home for breaking a man's arm. Mack had been with Randy during the robbery. Afterwards, he bragged that he had done the killing.

5. What did Jamal do well?
    He was good at drawing and painting.

6. Describe the discussion between Jamal and Dwayne.
    Dwayne insulted Jamal by criticizing his sneakers. Dwayne also said Jamal looked like a frog. Jamal threatened to put one of the sneakers upside Dwayne's head.

7. What were some of the things that made Jamal feel small inside?
    Dwayne, the man at the furniture store, teachers who called attention to him when he made a mistake or forgot his homework, big kids who laughed at him all made Jamal feel small.

Chapters 4-5

1. Who is Tito? What did he start to do right after he met Jamal?
    Tito is Jamal's best friend. He started borrowing Jamal's clothes soon after they met.

2. Did Jamal want to talk to Mack? Why or why not?
    No, he did not. He thought Mack was nothing but trouble.

3. How did Jamal feel about Randy? Why?
    He was mad at Randy because of the way Mama cried about his prison sentence. Jamal didn't like the cool way Randy looked when he heard the guilty verdict.

4. What did Mack tell Jamal about Randy?
    Randy's lawyer called him (Mack) and said he could make an appeal for two thousand dollars.

5. Why didn't the Scorpions want Randy out of jail?
   They thought he was too old. Younger boys would not have to testify if there were any trouble.

6. How did Mack suggest that Jamal get the money for Randy?
   Mack said Jamal should take over the Scorpions. Then they could make money by carrying for the Spanish guys.

Chapters 4-5 continued

7. How old is Jamal?
   He is twelve.

8. What did Jamal think Randy was doing to Mama?
   He was making her tired.

Chapters 6-7

1. Where did the boys go? What did they talk about?
   They went to the boat basin. They talked about the kind of boats they wanted to own. They asked a man about the price of the boats.

2. What disease/illness did Tito have? How did Jamal react to it?
   Tito had asthma. Jamal did not like it when Tito coughed, but he put his arm around Tito's shoulders. Later he told Tito that if they had money they could live in a warmer place where the asthma would not bother Tito.

3. What did Jamal do when he got home after the fight with Dwayne?
   He took off his ripped shirt and then put on the smaller of Randy's two Scorpions jackets.

4. What was Tito's reason for wanting to join the Scorpions?
   He thought he and Jamal could get the Scorpions to do some good.

5. What did Mack give to Jamal?
   Mack gave the gun to Jamal.

Chapters 8-9

1. How did Indian feel about having Jamal as the leader of the Scorpions?
   He thought Jamal was too young and inexperienced.

2. What did Angel say about Jamal leading the Scorpions?
   He said shooting and killing someone ran in the blood.

3. How did Jamal feel about Randy? About his father?
   He thought each of them had taken a bit of his mother that they could not return.

4. How did Jamal feel about the Scorpions?
   He was afraid of them. He was not sure if he wanted to join the gang. He did not want to have to fight Indian.

5. How did Jamal feel when his father left? Why?
   He felt bad, because his father made him feel like he should be doing something, but Jamal didn't know what it was.

6. Jamal thought something Dwayne did was not right. What was it?
   He thought Dwayne should not laugh at people.

Chapters 10-12
1. Describe the fight between Jamal and Dwayne
   They fought in the storeroom. They both landed some punches, and Jamal ripped Dwayne's shirt. Then Jamal pulled out the gun. He noticed Dwayne's fear, and Dwayne begged him not to shoot. Then Jamal put the gun back in the bag, and left the school building.

2. What was Jamal doing as he went down the stairs?
   He was crying.

3. Where did Tito and Jamal go when they left school? What did they do?
   They went down to the pier and shot the gun.

4. Describe the meeting between Jamal and Dwayne.
   Dwayne said he was thinking of telling the police about Jamal's gun. Jamal asked him if he wanted to mess with the Scorpions.

5. What kind of job did Jamal get?
   He worked in the bodega for Mr. Gonzalez. He stocked the shelves and carried groceries for customers.

6. Why was Tito crying?
   Abuela had found the gun and told him to leave the house.

7. What did Tito tell Abuela about the gun?
   He said he had found it at school.

8. What did Jamal tell himself he should do with the gun? Did he think he would do it?
   He told himself he should throw it away, but a part of him knew he would not.

Chapters 13-15
1. Describe the meeting with Jamal, Mr. Davidson, Dwayne, and Mrs. Parsons.
   Dwayne told them all about the gun. Mrs. Parsons wanted Mr. Davidson to call the police, but he said he could not do that unless he had proof that Jamal had a gun. Jamal denied having the gun. Mrs. Parsons said she was going to see a lawyer, and she left. Mr. Davidson said Jamal would have to sit in the lunchroom every day until his mother came to school.

2. Why did Mr. Davidson want to talk to Mrs. Hicks?
   He wanted to convince her to put Jamal in a school for problem students.

3. Where did Jamal go after the meeting?
   He left school.

4. What happened when Jamal got to Mr. Gonzalez's store?
    Indian and Angel were there waiting for him. Indian took some candy bars, then knocked over the dominoes on the table. Jamal thought he looked high. After they left, Mr. Gonzalez told Jamal to leave.

5. What happened to Randy?
    He had been stabbed while in prison.

6. How did Sassy find out about the gun? Did she tell Mama about it?
    She saw Darnell and he told her. No, she did not tell Mama about it.

7. What kind of sound did Mama make after she got home?
    It was like something big that was wounded.

8. Why didn't the Scorpions want Mack working with them?
    Mack would be tried and sentenced as an adult if he got caught again. The Scorpions only wanted younger boys who would not be in danger of doing time.

9. Describe Indian's plan, and Mack's ideas.
    Indian wanted to take over himself and keep the money. Mack wanted Jamal to work with him so they could use the money for Randy's appeal.

10. What was Jamal's decision about the gun?
    He decided to keep it a while longer, and possibly scare Indian with it.

<u>Chapters 16-17</u>
1. Jamal made a phone call to Indian. What did he say? What was the reply?
    Jamal talked to Angel, not Indian. He said that Randy had told his mother that Indian should be the leader, and the Scorpions should get the money for his appeal. Another voice got on and told Jamal to call back, because he had to make a call.

2. What message did Angel give when he called back?
    He said Indian wanted Jamal to meet him at the park the next night at eleven o'clock and tell all of the Scorpions what he had said on the phone earlier.

3. What was Jamal tell Tito he would do when he met Indian?
    He said if Indian started to beat him, he would take it and then walk away and go home, wash up, and laugh.

4. What did Mrs. Roberts want Jamal to do? Did he do it? Why or why not?
    She wanted him to take a form home and have his mother sign it. The form was a permission for the school to give Jamal medication to calm him down. Jamal agreed to do it, because it meant his mother would not have to meet with the principal.

5. Did Dwayne and Jamal fight?
    No, they did not.

6. What did Mama ask Mr. Stanton? What was his reply?
    She asked him to loan her the thousand dollars for a new trial for Randy. He said no.

7. What happened when Jamal and Tito met Indian and Angel in the park?
   Jamal told Indian and Angel that Randy said Indian was to be the leader. He also he was giving up the Scorpions' colors. Angel said he could not give up the colors unless the leader agreed. Then Angel and Indian started beating on Jamal. Angel pulled out a knife. Tito, who had been holding the gun, fired it. Angel fell to the ground and Indian crawled away. Tito and Jamal ran out of the park.

Chapters 18-20

1. What did the boys do with the gun?
   Jamal threw it in a dumpster.

2. What did Tito say was going to happen to him?
   He said God would punish him, that he would go to hell.

3. Jamal told Tito he could not come over for a week, because his mother was too upset about Randy. What was the real reason?
   Jamal was protecting Tito in case the Scorpions came to his house.

4. Where did Jamal and his family live?
   They lived in Harlem.

5. What did Mack tell Jamal?
   Mack told Jamal that he (Mack) had killed Angel and wounded Indian in the park the night before. He asked Jamal to take over the Scorpions, but Jamal talked Mack into taking the leadership. Mack agreed.

6. What happened to Tito?
   He told his grandmother about the gun, but said he had been alone. She got a lawyer, and they went to the police. The police charged Tito with being a juvenile delinquent, but said if he went back to Puerto Rico he would not be in trouble. Tito and his grandmother returned to Puerto Rico.

7. What did Jamal give Tito?
   Jamal gave Tito the portrait he had made.

MULTIPLE CHOICE STUDY/QUIZ QUESTIONS *Scorpions*

Chapters 1-3

1. Which statement about the characters is **false**?
    A. Jamal Hicks is a seventh grade boy.
    B. Randy is in jail for robbing a bank.
    C. Sassy is in the third grade.
    D. Mrs. Hicks works and tries to take care of the family.

2. True or False: Randy asked Mama for five hundred dollars so the lawyer could appeal his case.
    A. True
    B. False

3. What did Randy want Jamal to do?
    A. Randy wanted Jamal to be good and take care of their mother.
    B. Randy wanted Jamal to get a job and save up the money for an appeal.
    C. Randy wanted Jamal to start a new gang to fight the Scorpions.
    D. Randy wanted Jamal to go and see Mack.

4. True or False: Jamal looked up to Mack, and liked him a lot.
    A. True
    B. False

5. Which sentence about Mack is **true**?
    A. Mrs. Hicks liked him.
    B. Randy made him the temporary leader of the Scorpions.
    C. He had killed three members of another gang, but had not been caught.
    D. He had been in a juvenile home for breaking a man's arm.

6. What did Jamal do well?
    A. He was an excellent singer.
    B. He was very good at telling jokes.
    C. He was good at drawing and painting.
    D. He was a talented actor.

7. True or False: Dwayne insulted and criticized Jamal.
    A. True
    B. False

8. Which is **not** one of the things that made Jamal feel small inside?
    A. the man at the furniture store
    B. teachers who called attention to him when he made a mistake
    C. having a brother in jail
    D. big kids who laughed at him

Scorpions Multiple Choice Study Questions

Chapters 4-5

1. What did Tito start to do right after he met Jamal?
    - A. He started borrowing Jamal's clothes.
    - B. He started smoking.
    - C. He got his first girlfriend.
    - D. He started doing better in school.

2. Did Jamal want to talk to Mack?
    - A. Yes, he did.
    - B. No, he did not.

3. How did Jamal feel about Randy?
    - A. Jamal liked the cool way Randy looked when he heard the guilty verdict.
    - B. He thought his big brother was perfect.
    - C. He was mad at Randy because of the way Mama cried about his prison sentence.
    - D. Jamal did not like the tough-guy act that Randy always put on.

4. What did Mack tell Jamal about Randy?
    - A. Randy was going to try to escape in three days.
    - B. Randy was starting a new gang in prison.
    - C. Randy thought Jamal was a baby, and would never be able to help him.
    - D. Randy's lawyer said he could make an appeal for two thousand dollars.

5. True or False: Randy sent a message and resigned from the Scorpions.
    - A. True
    - B. False

6. Who thought up the following plan? Jamal would take over the Scorpions. Then they could make money by carrying for the Spanish guys.
    - A. Randy
    - B. Indian
    - C. Mack
    - D. Jamal

7. How old is Jamal?
    - A. He is fourteen.
    - B. He is seventeen.
    - C. He is fifteen.
    - D. He is twelve.

8. What did Jamal think Randy was doing to Mama?
    - A. He was making her tired.
    - B. He was stealing her money.
    - C. He was lying to her.
    - D. He was beating her.

Scorpions Multiple Choice Study Questions

Chapters 6-7

1. Tito and Jamal talked about something they both wanted to own. What was it?
    - A. They both wanted to buy big, beautiful houses for their families.
    - B. They both wanted to own boats.
    - C. They both wanted to own guns.
    - D. They both wanted to own fast sports cars.

2. How did Jamal react to Tito's asthma?
    - A. He thought Tito was faking so he would not have to run or fight.
    - B. He said he would try to earn money to get medicine for Tito.
    - C. He asked his mother to pray, because he was afraid Tito would die.
    - D. He wished they could live in a warmer place where it would not bother Tito.

3. What did Jamal do when he got home after the fight with Dwayne?
    - A. He put on the smaller of Randy's two Scorpions jackets.
    - B. He washed and mended his torn shirt.
    - C. He got a kitchen knife and put it in his belt.
    - D. He took a shower and cried.

4. True or False: Tito thought he and Jamal could get the Scorpions to do some good.
    - A. True
    - B. False

5. What did Mack give to Jamal?
    - A. Mack gave Jamal a set of brass knuckles.
    - B. Mack gave Jamal a bag of dope to deliver to someone else.
    - C. Mack gave Jamal five hundred dollars in cash.
    - D. Mack gave a gun to Jamal.

Scorpions Multiple Choice Study Questions

Chapters 8-9

1. Who thought Jamal was too young and inexperienced to lead the Scorpions?
   - A. Marcus
   - B. Indian
   - C. Tito
   - D. Bobby

2. Who said shooting and killing someone ran in the blood?
   - A. Randy
   - B. Mack
   - C. Angel
   - D. Jevon

3. True or False: Jamal thought the troubles with her husband and Randy had made his mother a very strong woman.
   - A. True
   - B. False

4. True or False: Jamal was not sure if he wanted to join the Scorpions.
   - A. True
   - B. False

5. How did Jamal feel when his father left?
   - A. He hated his father and was glad to see him go.
   - B. He felt angry because his father was not helping the family enough.
   - C. He felt like he should be doing something, but didn't know what it was.
   - D. He loved his father and wanted him to stay.

6. Jamal thought something Dwayne did was not right. What was it?
   - A. He thought Dwayne should not cheat on tests.
   - B. He thought Dwayne should not be so mean to the girls.
   - C. he thought Dwayne should stop stealing money from the teachers' desks.
   - D. He thought Dwayne should not laugh at people.

Scorpions Multiple Choice Study Questions

Chapters 10-12

1. True or False: Jamal pulled the gun on Dwayne while they were fighting.
    A. True
    B. False

2. What was Jamal doing as he went down the stairs?
    A. He was cursing.
    B. He was crying.
    C. He was singing.
    D. He was sliding down on the railing.

3. Where did Tito and Jamal go when they left school? What did they do?
    A. They went to the church and went to confession.
    B. They went out and had pizza.
    C. They buried the gun in a hole behind Tito's house.
    D. They went down to the pier and shot the gun.

4. True or False: Dwayne went right to the police and told them about the gun.
    A. True
    B. False

5. What kind of job did Jamal get?
    A. He started babysitting for a woman with five children.
    B. He pumped gas and washed cars at a gas station.
    C. He worked in the bodega, stocking the shelves and carrying groceries.
    D. He cleaned office buildings with his mother.

6. True or False: Abuela found the gun and told Tito to leave the house.
    A. True
    B. False

7. What did Tito tell Abuela about the gun?
    A. He told her it belonged to Jamal.
    B. He said he bought it to protect her.
    C. He said his father had sent it to him.
    D. He said he had found it at school.

8. Did Jamal believe he would really throw away the gun?
    A. Yes, he did.
    B. No, he did not.

Scorpions Multiple Choice Study Questions

Chapters 13-15

1. Which did **not** happen during the meeting with Jamal, Mr. Davidson, Dwayne, and Mrs. Parsons.
    A. Mrs. Parsons wanted Mr. Davidson to call the police.
    B. Jamal denied having the gun.
    C. Mr. Davidson suspended both boys for fighting in school.
    D. Mrs. Parsons said she was going to see a lawyer.

2. Why did Mr. Davidson want to talk to Mrs. Hicks?
    A. He wanted to convince her to put Jamal in a school for problem students.
    B. He wanted to help with Randy's appeal.
    C. He wanted to have her put Jamal in a foster home for a while.
    D. He wanted to send both of them to a social worker.

3. True or False: Jamal went to see Randy after the meeting.
    A. True
    B. False

4. Why did Jamal get fired from his job?
    A. Mr. Gonzalez had heard about the gun.
    B. He was late and was not doing all of his work.
    C. He stole money from the cash register.
    D. Indian and Angel came in and caused trouble.

5. What happened to Randy?
    A. He tried to escape and was shot.
    B. He successfully escaped and was on the run.
    C. He had been stabbed while in prison.
    D. He got time taken off his sentence for good behavior.

6. Did Sassy tell Mama about the gun?
    A. Yes, she did.
    B. No, she did not.

7. What kind of sound did Mama make after she got home?
    A. It was like something big that was wounded.
    B. She made a very loud scream.
    C. She laughed so hard she started to cry.
    D. She did not make any sound at all.

8. True or False: The Scorpions only wanted younger boys who would not be in danger of doing time.
    A. True
    B. False

9. Who wanted to take over the Scorpions himself and keep the money?
    A. Garvey
    B. Angel
    C. Bobby
    D. Indian

10. True or False: Jamal gave the gun back to Mack.
    A. True
    B. False

Scorpions Multiple Choice Study Questions

<u>Chapters 16-17</u>
1. What was Jamal's phone message to Indian?
   A. Jamal said he would take Indian out if he opposed having Jamal be the leader.
   B. He said that Randy had told his mother that Indian should be the leader, and the Scorpions should get the money for his appeal.
   C. Jamal said he was too young to be a Scorpion. If they would leave him alone, he would leave them alone.
   D. Jamal said he was giving the gun back to Mack, and that Mack should be the leader.

2. What message did Angel give when he called back?
   A. He said Indian accepted his offer.
   B. He said Indian did not believe him and wanted to fight.
   C. He said Indian wanted Jamal to meet him at the park the next night at eleven o'clock and tell all of the Scorpions what he had said on the phone earlier.
   D. He said Indian was taking over immediately. If Jamal ever came around the Scorpions or their clubhouse, he would be killed immediately.

3. What did Jamal tell Tito he would do when he met Indian?
   A. He would use the gun and shoot to kill.
   B. Nothing. He was planning to stay away from Indian.
   C. He would try to talk to Indian without fighting.
   D. He would take it and then walk away and go home, wash up, and laugh.

4. Mrs. Roberts gave Jamal a form to have signed. What was it about?
   A. It was a permission for the school to give Jamal medication to calm him down.
   B. It gave the principal permission to hit Jamal if he misbehaved.
   C. It was a transfer to another school.
   D. It gave the school permission to keep Jamal in the same grade the next year.

5. Did Dwayne and Jamal fight?
   A. Yes, they did.
   B. No, they did not.

6. Mama asked Mr. Stanton to loan her the money for the appeal. What was his reply?
   A. He said yes.
   B. He said no.

7. Which event did **not** happened when Jamal and Tito met Indian and Angel in the park?
   A. Jamal told Indian and Angel that Randy said Indian was to be the leader.
   B. Indian told Jamal he was expelled from the Scorpions.
   C. Angel and Indian started beating on Jamal.
   D. Angel pulled out a knife.

8. Who fired the gun?
   A. Angel
   B. Jamal
   C. Tito
   D. Mack

Scorpions Multiple Choice Study Questions

<u>Chapters 18-20</u>
1. What did the boys do with the gun?
    A. Jamal threw it in a dumpster.
    B. They buried it under a bush in the park.
    C. They threw it in the river.
    D. Jamal kept it.

2. What did Tito say was going to happen to him?
    A. He said he would spend the rest of his life in jail.
    B. He said God would punish him, that he would go to hell.
    C. He said his grandmother would throw him out for good.
    D. He said his father would beat him.

3. Jamal told Tito he could not come over for a week, because his mother was too upset about Randy. What was the real reason?
    A. Jamal wanted to forget about everything that had happened.
    B. Jamal did not want Tito to see how upset he was.
    C. Jamal's mother found out about the gun and said he could not see Tito.
    D. Jamal was protecting Tito in case the Scorpions came to his house.

4. Where did Jamal and his family live?
    A. They lived in West Philadelphia.
    B. They lived in Harlem.
    C. They lived in Watts.
    D. They lived in Detroit.

5. True or False: Mack told Jamal that he (Mack) had killed Angel and wounded Indian in the park the night before.
    A. True
    B. False

6. What happened to Tito?
    A. He was sent to reform school for three years.
    B. Tito and his grandmother returned to Puerto Rico.
    C. He ran away and was never heard from again.
    D. Nothing. The lawyer said it was self defense and there were no charges.

7. What did Jamal give Tito?
    A. Jamal gave Tito the gun to keep.
    B. Jamal gave Tito one of the Scorpions jackets.
    C. Jamal gave Tito the portrait he had made.
    D. Jamal gave Tito a hug.

ANSWER KEY: MULTIPLE CHOICE/QUIZ QUESTIONS *Scorpions*

Chapters 1-3	Chapters 4-5	Chapters 6-7	Chapters 8-9
1. B	1. A	1. B	1. B
2. A TRUE	2. B	2. D	2. C
3. D	3. C	3. A	3. B FALSE
4. B FALSE	4. D	4. A TRUE	4. A TRUE
5. D	5. B FALSE	5. D	5. C
6. C	6. C		6. D
7. A	7. D		
8. C	8. A		

Chapters 10-12	Chapters 13-15	Chapters 16-17	Chapters 18-20
1. A TRUE	1. C	1. B	1. A
2. B	2. A	2. C	2. B
3. D	3. B FALSE	3. D	3. D
4. B FALSE	4. D	4. A	4. B
5. C	5. C	5. B	5. A TRUE
6. A TRUE	6. B	6. B	6. B
7. D	7. A	7. B	7. C
8. B	8. A TRUE	8. C	
	9. D		
	10. B FALSE		

STUDENT ANSWER SHEET-MULTIPLE CHOICE/QUIZ QUESTIONS

Chapters 1-3	Chapters 4-5	Chapters 6-7	Chapters 8-9
1.	1.	1.	1.
2.	2.	2.	2.
3.	3.	3.	3.
4.	4.	4.	4.
5.	5.	5.	5.
6.	6.		6.
7.	7.		
8.	8.		

Chapters 10-12	Chapters 13-15	Chapters 16-17	Chapters 18-20
1.	1.	1.	1.
2.	2.	2.	2.
3.	3.	3.	3.
4.	4.	4.	4.
5.	5.	5.	5.
6.	6.	6.	6.
7.	7.	7.	7.
8.	8.	8.	
	9.		
	10.		

VOCABULARY WORKSHEETS

VOCABULARY WORKSHEETS *Scorpions*

Chapters 1-3
Part I: Using Prior Knowledge and Context Clues

Below are the sentences in which the vocabulary words appear in the text. Read the sentence. Use any clues you can find in the sentence combined with your prior knowledge, and write what you think the underlined words mean in the space provided.

1. "Why don't you go down to the ***subway***?" "Suppose she come on the bus or take a taxi?"

2. "He talking about how he gonna ***appeal*** his case and stuff, and asking me if I got five hundred dollars."

3. Randy got fifteen to twenty years, and the lawyer said that he would have to stay in for at least seven years before he could come out on ***parole***.

4. The summer before Randy had got into trouble, Mack had been in ***juvenile*** home for breaking a man's arm with a baseball bat.

5. "He gonna mess around," the dark, ***squat*** woman said, "and they gonna put that murder right on him."

Part II: Determining the Meaning   Match the vocabulary words to their dictionary definitions.

1. subway   A. supervised freedom from prison
2. appeal   B. low and broad
3. parole   C. for or about children or young people
4. juvenile   D. a request for a new court hearing
5. squat   E. an underground, electric railway

Scorpions Vocabulary Worksheets

Chapters 4-5
Part I: Using Prior Knowledge and Context Clues
Below are the sentences in which the vocabulary words appear in the text. Read the sentence. Use any clues you can find in the sentence combined with your prior knowledge, and write what you think the underlined words mean in the space provided.

1. The teenager looked at him *sullenly*, then walked slowly on.

2. A short, *stocky* man with a square head, dressed in a gray suit and a pink shirt, started into the store, then stopped and walked over to Jamal and Tito.

3. "They got Willie on *possession*, and then he tried to cop him a plea by turning Randy and me."

4. Jamal watched a group of pigeons *strut* around a half-eaten corn muffin on the ground.

5. Some jive stuff about how he was too *slick* for the police.

Part II: Determining the Meaning Match the vocabulary words to their dictionary definitions.

1. sullenly   A. shrewd; tricky
2. stocky   B. solidly built; sturdy
3. possession   C. a swaggering walk
4. strut   D. with silent resentment
5. slick   E. holding without ownership

Scorpions Vocabulary Worksheets

Chapters 6-7
Part I: Using Prior Knowledge and Context Clues
Below are the sentences in which the vocabulary words appear in the text. Read the sentence. Use any clues you can find in the sentence combined with your prior knowledge, and write what you think the underlined words mean in the space provided.

1. When he coughed really hard, Tito's eyes would roll around and ***glisten*** with his efforts.

2. The boys watched as he went about the boat checking things, then climbed over the side onto the ***pier***.

3. Jamal smiled and looked at the boat. . . . "It's not really my ***yacht***," the man said.

4. In science they saw a movie. It was about water ***pollution***.

Part II Determine the Meaning Match the vocabulary words to their dictionary definitions.

1. glisten   A. a small boat used for cruises or racing
2. pier   B. shine
3. yacht   C. harmful waste matter
4. pollution   D. a platform over the water

Scorpions Vocabulary Worksheets

Chapters 8-9
Part I: Using Prior Knowledge and Context Clues
Below are the sentences in which the vocabulary words appear in the text. Read the sentence. Use any clues you can find in the sentence combined with your prior knowledge, and write what you think the underlined words mean in the space provided.

1. When they passed some shops on 125th Street, Jamal saw their ***reflections*** in the windows.

2. Over the window there was a picture of a small gold ***shield*** with a black scorpion on it.

3. He had a narrow face, with thin ***slits*** for eyes.

4. All he remembered was a few times when his father had taken him under one arm and Sassy under the other and run around the park outside the ***projects*** where they used to live.

Part II: Determining the Meaning   Match the vocabulary words to their dictionary definitions.

1. reflections   A. images
2. shield   B. government funded housing for the poor
3. slits   C. long, narrow openings
4. projects   D. a piece of armor strapped to the arm

Draw a picture of the Scorpions' shield.

Scorpions Vocabulary Worksheets

Chapters 10-12
Part I: Using Prior Knowledge and Context Clues
Below are the sentences in which the vocabulary words appear in the text. Read the sentence. Use any clues you can find in the sentence combined with your prior knowledge, and write what you think the underlined words mean in the space provided.

1. Jamal **glanced** over to where Tamita Davis leaned against the wall.

2. The inside of the storeroom was **musty**.

3. Dwayne came at him again, **bobbing** and weaving like a boxer.

4. His leg was hurting, and he **stumbled** as he went down the stairs.

5. The two women got on one of the boats and went into the little **compartment.**

Part II: Determining the Meaning   Match the vocabulary words to their dictionary definitions.

1. glanced   A. tripped
2. musty   B. stale or moldy
3. bobbing   C. moving up and down
4. stumbled   D. a small room or section
5. compartment   E. gazed briefly

* Not tested: Mama said that she had gone to a different **bodega** on the avenue to get some **plantains**, and that the guy who owned it, Mr. Gonzalez, said he needed someone to help out in the afternoons.
bodega--(Spanish) a small grocery store
plantain-- a fruit resembling a banana, but firmer. It is often served fried.

Scorpions Vocabulary Worksheets

Chapters 13-15
Part I: Using Prior Knowledge and Context Clues
Below are the sentences in which the vocabulary words appear in the text. Read the sentence.
Use any clues you can find in the sentence combined with your prior knowledge, and write what you think the underlined words mean in the space provided.

1. He had remembered, **_vaguely_**, Mr. Hunter talking about those wars, but they hadn't sounded very interesting.

2. "It's not the school's position to make **_hasty_** accusations," Mr. Davidson said.

3. "It's not the school's position to make hasty **_accusations_**," Mr. Davidson said.

4. "Maybe put you some place for kids with serious problems, or someplace that you're not going to **_contaminate_** everybody else."

5. Jamal had heard that in the back, behind the ply board and the curtains, there was a room made of steel where the crack dealers put the crack in little **_vials_**.

Part II: Matching   Match the vocabulary words to their dictionary definitions.

1. vaguely   A. small containers with stoppers
2. hasty   B. to make impure
3. accusations   C. not clearly expressed
4. contaminate   D. charges of wrongdoing
5. vials   E. rapidly; quickly

Scorpions Vocabulary Worksheets

Chapters 16-17
Part I: Using Prior Knowledge and Context Clues
Below are the sentences in which the vocabulary words appear in the text. Read the sentence. Use any clues you can find in the sentence combined with your prior knowledge, and write what you think the underlined words mean in the space provided.

1. The voice on the other end of the phone was **_gravelly_** as he called Indian's name out loud.

2. Neither one said anything while they watched an **_episode_** of Thunder Cats that they both had seen before.

3. "The lawyer say if he hurt in there, then they get **_anxious_** to get him out so they don't have to take care of him."

4. It was all over Mama's face, in the sadness of her eyes and in the way her shoulders **_drooped_** before she sat down.

5. Mama looked at Jamal and **_beckoned_** him over to her.

6. The **_aroma_** of their perfume lingered in the air behind them.

7. The aroma of their perfume **_lingered_** in the air behind them.

8. Jamal stood still, trying to **_peer_** through the darkness, trying to ignore the shadows of the trees that moved before him.

Part II: Determining the Meaning   Match the vocabulary words to their dictionary definitions.

1. gravelly   A. fearful; panicky
2. episode   B. persisted; stayed
3. anxious   C. sounding harsh or rasping
4. drooped   D. a pleasant odor
5. beckoned   E. to look or search
6. aroma   F. bent or sagged downward
7. lingered   G. one part of a serial story or show
8. peer   H. made a signaling gesture

Scorpions Vocabulary Worksheets

Chapters 18-20
Part I: Using Prior Knowledge and Context Clues
Below are the sentences in which the vocabulary words appear in the text. Read the sentence.
Use any clues you can find in the sentence combined with your prior knowledge, and write what
you think the underlined words mean in the space provided.

1. They ran out of the far end of the park, past the darkened ***tenements***, until they couldn't run anymore.

2. Billy ***stammered*** and looked around, and Jamal figured that he had said the same things to both of them.

3. "I've seen you acting kind of ***droopy*** this week," Mama said. "You ain't using that dope, are you?"

4. Jamal's stomach ***clenched*** when he saw him sitting on the stoop.

5. Jamal's stomach clenched when he saw him sitting on the ***stoop***.

6. Jamal's legs nearly gave way, and he sat down on the ***bannister***.

7. "Unh-uh. They called the school to make sure how old I was, and they charged me with being a juvenile ***delinquent***."

Part II: Determining the Meaning   Match the vocabulary words to their dictionary definitions.

1. tenements   A. a handrail
2. stammered   B. closed tightly
3. droopy   C. spoke with involuntary pauses
4. clenched   D. a building's small porch or staircase
5. stoop   E. sagging in exhaustion
6. bannister   F. someone who disobeys the law
7. delinquent   G. run-down apartment buildings

ANSWER KEY-PREREADING VOCABULARY WORKSHEETS

Chapters 1-3
1. E
2. D
3. A
4. C
5. B

Chapters 4-5
1. D
2. B
3. E
4. C
5. A

Chapters 6-7
1. B
2. D
3. A
4. C

Chapters 8-9
1. A
2. D
3. C
4. B

Chapters 10-12
1. E
2. B
3. C
4. A
5. D

Chapters 13-15
1. C
2. E
3. D
4. B
5. A

Chapters 16-17
1. C
2. G
3. A
4. F
5. H
6. D
7. B
8. E

Chapters 18-20
1. G
2. C
3. E
4. B
5. D
6. A
7. F

DAILY LESSONS

LESSON ONE

Student Objectives
1. To preview the *Scorpions Unit*
2. To receive books and other related materials
3. To relate prior knowledge to the new material
4. To become familiar with the vocabulary for Chapters 1-3
5. To preview the study questions for Chapters 1-3

Activity #1

Ask students to share information they know about gangs, teen violence, or life in urban areas. Tell them the story they are going to read a story about a boy who lives in an urban area, and has dealings with a gang.

Activity #2

Distribute the materials students will use in this unit. Explain in detail how students are to use these materials.

Study Guides Students should preview the study guide questions before each reading assignment to get a feeling for what events and ideas are important in that section. After reading the section, students will (as a class or individually) answer the questions to review the important events and ideas from that section of the book. Students should keep the study guides as study materials for the unit test.

Reading Assignment Sheet You need to fill in the reading assignment sheet to let students know when their reading has to be completed. You can either write the assignment sheet on a side blackboard or bulletin board and leave it there for students to see each day, or you can duplicate copies for each student to have. In either case, you should advise students to become very familiar with the reading assignments so they know what is expected of them.

Unit Outline You may find it helpful to distribute copies of the Unit Outline to your students so they can keep track of upcoming lessons and assignments. You may also want to post a copy of the Unit Outline on a bulletin board and cross off each lesson as you complete it.

Extra Activities Center The Unit Resource portion of this unit contains suggestions for a library of related books and articles in your classroom as well as crossword and word search puzzles. Make an extra activities center in your room where you will keep these materials for students to use. Bring the books and articles in from the library and keep several copies of the puzzles on hand. Explain to students that these materials are available for students to use when they finish reading assignments or other class work early.

Books Each school has its own rules and regulations regarding student use of school books. Advise students of the procedures that are normal for your school.

Notebook or Unit Folder You may want the students to keep all of their worksheets, notes, and other papers for the unit together in a binder or notebook. During the first class meeting, tell them how you want them to arrange the folder. Make divider pages for vocabulary worksheets, prereading study guide questions, review activities, notes, and tests. You may want to give a grade for accuracy in keeping the folder.

Activity #3

Do a group KWL Sheet (p. 49) with the students. Some students will know something about Walter Dean Myers and/or *Scorpions*, and will have information to share. Put this information in the K column (What I Know.) Ask students what they want to find out from reading the book and record this in the W column (What I Want to Find Out.) Keep the sheet and refer back to it after reading the book. Complete the L column (What I Learned) at that time.

Activity #4

Work through the prereading vocabulary worksheet for Chapters 1-3 with the students. Tell them they will have a sheet like this to complete before reading each section of the book.

Activity #5

Show students how to preview the study questions for Chapters 1-3 of *Scorpions*. Encourage students to predict what they think answers might be, to write down their predictions, and to compare these with their answers after reading the chapters.

KWL *Scorpions*

Directions: Before reading, think about what you already know about Walter Dean Myers and/or *Scorpions*. Write the information in the K column. Think about what you would like to find out from reading the book. Write your questions in the W column. After you have read the book, use the L column to write the answers to your questions from the W column, and anything else you remember from the book.

K What I Know	W What I Want To Find Out	L What I Learned

LESSON TWO

Objectives
1. To discuss the main ideas and events in Chapters 1-3
2. To begin Writing Assignment #1-Journal Writing

Activity #1

Discuss the answers to the Study Guide questions for Chapters 1-3 in detail. Write the answers on the board or overhead projector so students can have the correct answers for study purposes. Encourage students to take notes. If the students own their books, encourage them to use highlighter pens to mark important passages and the answers to the study guide questions.

Note: It is a good practice in public speaking and leadership skills for individual students to take charge of leading the discussion of the study questions. Perhaps a different student could go to the front of the class and lead the discussion each day that the study questions are discussed during this unit. Of course, the teacher should guide the discussion when appropriate and be sure to fill in any gaps the students leave.

Activity #2

Tell students they will be keeping a sketchbook- journal as Writing Assignment #1, Writing to Express a Personal Opinion. Explain that a sketchbook- journal is a combination of sketches about and written responses to the story. They will be required to make an entry for each chapter in the novel.

Students can sketch memorable scenes from the chapters, or paste in magazine pictures that remind them of the events in the chapter.

The written entries should focus on each student's response to the literature, and should not merely be a plot summary. They should include comments about their thoughts and feelings while reading, any questions they have, and predictions for the next chapter.

It is up to the individual teacher to decide how to grade or respond to the journals, and whether to have students share them with the class or keep them private.

Distribute copies of Writing Assignment #1(p. 51) and go over it in detail with the students. Assign a due date for completing the journal. The remainder of the lessons in this lesson plan guide allot some time each day for students to work in their journals.

WRITING ASSIGNMENT #1 *Scorpions*
Journal Writing to Express a Personal Opinion

PROMPT

For this unit, you will be asked to keep a sketchbook- journal. This is a combination of sketches about and written responses to a story. You will be required to make an entry for each chapter in the novel.

First, decide on the format for your sketchbook-journal. Spend some time decorating your cover and setting up the book. Make sure to include the title of each chapter and the page numbers in you copy of the book. Also date each entry.

You can sketch memorable scenes from the chapters, paste in magazine pictures , or use computer clip art.. Even if you do not consider yourself a good artist, try to make some sketches. Use colors that remind you of the mood of the story. You may want to take photographs and put them in the sketchbook-journal.

The written entries should focus on your response to the literature, and should not merely be chapter summaries. They should include comments about your thoughts and feelings while reading, any questions you have, and predictions about the next chapter. Try to write at least one page for each entry. You, your class mates and your teacher will decide whether to share the journals or keep them private.

Here are some suggestions for the types of entries you may want to make.

Check Your Understanding	Explain how the story is making sense to you. Give examples and note page numbers. Establish the setting, mood, point of view, and character relationships. Discuss the stated themes.
Make Inferences	Explain your thoughts about the feelings and motives of the characters. Discuss the implied themes.
Make and Revise Predictions	At the end of each chapter, make a prediction about what you think will happen next. After you read, go back and check your predictions. Tell if you had to revise them, and why.
Ask Questions	Ask questions about scenes or events that are confusing. Record the answers if you discuss the questions in class, or later find the answer in the novel.
Give Your Opinion	Give your opinion about the literary quality of the work. Discuss the author's style, use of language, and use of literary devices. Tell why you do nor do not like the story. Tell how you feel while reading the chapters. Compare the book with others you have read.

Make Connections   Think about ways the characters and events relate to your own life and experiences. Put yourself in the character's place and discuss how you would think or feel in that situation. Try this from the point of view of the main character and a few of the minor ones.

Make Recommendations   Tell what you think the characters should do or say. Tell how you would end the story, or what you think might happen next.

LESSON THREE

Objectives
1. To become familiar with the vocabulary for Chapters 4-5
2. To preview the study questions for Chapters 4-5
3. To read Chapters 4-5
4. To identify conflicts in the novel so far
5. To record thoughts and ideas in the journal

Activity #1 Minilesson: Conflict

Tell students that conflict is one of the most important aspects of a work of fiction. The conflict usually is an obstacle to the main character's goal. It usually brings about some type of change in the main character. The types of conflict that are evident in *Scorpions* are character vs. character, character vs. himself, and character vs. society.

You may want to use examples from stories the students have previously read, or examples from literature for younger children to illustrate the various types of conflict. Dorothy in *The Wizard of Oz* has a conflict with nature because the tornado takes her away from her home. The conflict between Cinderella and her wicked step-mother is an example of character vs. character. In *The Little Engine That Could*, the little engine is not sure of its ability to take the train over the mountain, illustrating the character vs. himself conflict. The Greek myth of Atalanta illustrates character vs. society or the environment. Atalanta was expected to marry the man her father chose, but she did not wish to do so.

Have students begin filling out the Conflict Chart (p. 53) after they have read Chapters 4-5. Discuss their findings. Encourage them to look for more examples of conflict as they read. Tell them they will discuss conflict again in Lesson Fourteen.

Activity #3

Give students about ten or fifteen minutes to do the prereading vocabulary work and preview the study questions for Chapters 4-5.

Activity #4

Have students begin reading Chapters 4 and 5. Depending on the needs and abilities of your students, either have them read silently or orally.

Activity #5

Give students a few minutes to make journal entries, or remind them to work on their journals outside of class time.

CONFLICT CHART

Directions: Use the chart below to record examples of the different types of conflict you read about in *Scorpions*.

CONFLICT	EXAMPLE & PAGES	CHANGE IN CHARACTER
CHARACTER VS. NATURE		
CHARACTER VS. SELF		
CHARACTER VS. SOCIETY		
CHARACTER VS. CHARACTER		

LESSON FOUR

Student Objectives
1. To discuss the main ideas and events in Chapters 4-5
2. To become familiar with the vocabulary for Chapters 6-7
3. To preview the study questions for Chapters 6-7
4. To identify examples of dialect in the novel
5. To read Chapters 6-7
6. To record thoughts and ideas in the journal

Activity #1

Have students work with a partner and go over their study guide questions and answers for Chapters 4-5. Then briefly go over the answers with the whole class.

Activity #2

Give students ten or fifteen minutes to complete the prereading vocabulary worksheet and go over the study guide questions.

Activity #3 Minilesson: Dialect

Tell students that dialect is a form of speech that is characteristic of a certain geographical region or group of people. Ethnic, social, and occupational groups often have their own dialects. Dialect varies from the standard language in its pronunciation, grammar, vocabulary, and syntax (word order in sentences.) There is no right or wrong dialect. Most TV and radio announces speak the dialect that is usually referred to as Standard English. This is also the format used for most writing.

For example, people in different areas have different names for a sandwich made on a large roll, including grinder (New England) hoagie (New Jersey and Northeastern Pennsylvania) sub (Middle Atlantic and West coast) and po'boy (southeastern United States.)

Geographic areas have different pronunciations. Ask students who were born in various areas to pronounce words such as *water* or *merry*. The class should be able to hear slight differences in the pronunciation of the vowels.

Non-native speakers sometimes transfer characteristics of their original language when they speak English. Spanish speakers who are accustomed to putting the adjective after the noun may say "station-train" instead of *train station*. Speakers of other languages may add or delete adjectives, depending on their use in the native language.

Writers often use dialect to add a regional or ethnic flavor to their writing. Authors such as Mark Twain (*The Adventures of Tom Sawyer, Huckleberry Finn*) and Zora Neal Hurston (*Their Eyes Were Watching God*) effectively used dialect in their novels.

Walter Dean Myers uses dialect in the conversations among the characters in the novel. Ask students to look find examples of dialect in the chapters of *Scorpions* that they have read so far. Discuss its effectiveness in the novel.

Some examples:

Ch. 1 "You the one who always want to watch it," Jamal said. (The word *are* is omitted after *you*; final *s* is omitted on the word *want*.)

Ch. 8: "He got a piece!" (The word *piece* is used instead of the word *gun*.)

Activity #4
    Give students the rest of the class period to read the assigned chapters. Remind them that the chapters must be read before the next class period.

Activity #5
    Give students a few minutes to make journal entries, or remind them to work on their journals outside of class time.

LESSON FIVE

Objectives
    1. To discuss the main ideas and events in Chapters 6-7
    2. To become familiar with the vocabulary for Chapters 8-9
    3. To preview the study questions for Chapters 8-9
    4. To read Chapters 8-9 orally for evaluation
    5. To record thoughts and ideas in the journal

Activity # 1
    Give each student four 1"x2" strips of colored paper or index cards--one blue, one yellow, one green, one pink. Have them put a large letter A on the blue paper, B on the yellow, C on the green, and D on the pink. Distribute copies of the Multiple Choice/Quiz questions for Chapters 6-7. Ask students to read the first question and hold up the colored paper for the correct answer. Then have them mark the correct answer on their worksheets.

Activity #2
    Give students ten or fifteen minutes to complete the prereading vocabulary worksheet and go over the study guide questions for Chapters 8-9.

Activity #3
    Tell students their oral reading ability will be evaluated. Show them copies of the Oral Reading Evaluation Form (p. 56) and discuss it. Model correct intonation and expression by reading the first few paragraphs of Chapter 6 aloud.

Activity #4
    Call on individual students to read a few paragraphs aloud. Encourage the other students to follow along silently in their books. If you have a student who is unwilling or unable to read in front of the group make arrangements to do his or her evaluation privately at another time.

Activity #5
    Give students a few minutes to make journal entries, or remind them to work on their journals outside of class time.

LESSON SIX

Objectives
1. To discuss the main ideas and events in Chapters 8-9
2. To identify figurative language in the novel.

Activity #1

Divide the class into six groups and have each group prepare the answer to one study guide question. Have a spokesperson from each group present the answer.

Activity #2 Minilesson: Figurative Language

Figures of speech are literary devices that give the writer a non-literal way to describe images and events. You may want to make a transparency of page 57 and use it to give examples of the different figures of speech. Then write *Sassy was eight, and coffee colored like her father* on the board. (This description is in Chapter Two.) Ask students to identify the two figures of speech. (*Coffee-colored* is a metaphor; *like her father* is a simile.) Talk about the literal meanings. Distribute the Figure of Speech worksheet (p. 58) and have students work in small groups to find examples in the novel. If you want the students to continue recording examples in the remaining chapters, assign a due date for the worksheet.

Activity # 3

Tell students they will have a quiz on Chapters 1-9 during the next class period.

ORAL READING EVALUATION *Scorpions*

Name_____   Class_____ Date_____

Title of Book: _____   Pages Read: _____

SKILL	EXCELLENT	GOOD	AVERAGE	FAIR	POOR
FLUENCY	5	4	3	2	1
CLARITY	5	4	3	2	1
AUDIBILITY	5	4	3	2	1
PRONUNCIATION	5	4	3	2	1
_____	5	4	3	2	1
_____	5	4	3	2	1

TOTAL   _____

GRADE   _____

COMMENTS:

FIGURES OF SPEECH

CLICHÉ   A cliché is an expression that has been used repeatedly, and has lost its appeal. For example: *white as snow, bright and early.*

HYPERBOLE   Extreme exaggeration used to describe a person or thing. For example: *She had as many pairs of shoes as there are stars in the sky.*

IRONY   The use of words to express something different from and often opposite to their literal meaning.

METAPHOR   A comparison without the words like or as. For example, *The cat is a bag of bones.*

METONYMY   A figure of speech in which one word or phrase is substituted for another with which it is closely associated, as in the use of *Washington* for the United States government or of *the sword* for military power.

ONOMATOPOEIA   The use of words such as *buzz* or *splash* that imitate the sounds associated with the objects or actions they refer to.

PARADOX   A seemingly self-contradictory statement that has some truth to it.

PERSONIFICATION   Attributing human characteristics to inanimate objects, animals, or ideas, as in *the wind howled.*

SIMILE   A comparison using the words like or as. *She is as pretty as a rose.*

FIGURES OF SPEECH

Figures of speech are literary devices that give the writer a non-literal way to describe images and events. The main types of figures of speech are hyperbole, irony, metaphor, metonymy, onomatopoeia, paradox, personification, and simile. Use the following chart to record examples of figures of speech used in *Scorpions*. A sample has been done for you. Note: You may not find an example of each figure of speech in the novel.

Figure of Speech	Example from Novel & Page #	Literal Meaning
coffee colored	Chapter 2, p. 9	Sassy's skin is the same shade of brown as coffee

LESSON SEVEN

Objectives
1. To take a quiz on Chapters 1-9
2. To become familiar with the vocabulary for Chapters 10-12
4. To preview the study questions for Chapters 10-12
5. To read Chapters 10-12
6. To record thoughts and ideas in the journal

Activity #1
Quiz--distribute quizzes (multiple choice study questions for Chapters 1-9) and give students about fifteen minutes to complete them. Collect the papers for scoring and recording the grades.

Activity #2
Give students about fifteen minutes to do the prereading vocabulary worksheet and study guide questions for Chapters 10-12. You may want to let them work with a partner or in small groups for this activity.

Activity #3
Give students a few minutes to make journal entries, or remind them to work on their journals outside of class time.

LESSON EIGHT

Objectives
1. To write a persuasive essay

Activity #1
Distribute copies of Writing Assignment #2 (p. 60.) Go over the assignment in detail with the students. Tell them they will have the remainder of the class period to begin working on the assignment. Give the due date for the completed assignment. It should be a few days before the writing conferences, which are scheduled for Lesson Twelve.

Activity #2
Distribute copies of the Writing Evaluation Form (p. 61) Explain to students that during Lesson Twelve you will be holding individual writing conferences about this writing assignment. Make sure students are familiar with the criteria on the Writing Evaluation Form.

Follow Up: After you have graded the assignments, have a writing conference with each student. This Unit Plan schedules one in Lesson Twelve. After the writing conference, allow students to revise their papers using your suggestions to complete the revisions. Grade the revisions on an A-C-E scale: A = all revisions well done; C = some revisions made; E = few or no revisions made. This will speed your grading time and still give some credit for the students' efforts.

WRITING ASSIGNMENT #2 *Scorpions*
Persuasive

PROMPT

Mack gave the gun to Jamal, and Jamal wore the gun to his meeting with the Scorpions. Later on, he threatened Dwayne with the gun during a fight. Tito and Jamal both shot the gun down by the water. The boys had mixed feelings about having the gun. Tito wanted to get rid of it, but Jamal was not sure.

You and a partner will take the roles of Jamal and Tito. Together you will write a dialog about the gun. If you write as Tito, you will be in favor of getting rid of it. If you write as Jamal, you will be in favor of keeping it.

The two of you may want to role-play and talk through your arguments before you write them down.

PREWRITING

Make a list of the reasons for your position. Think of statements to support each of your reasons, and list them under each reason. Then number the reasons in order from most to least important.

DRAFTING

You and your partner should work together on the draft. Put the speaker's name to the left of each line of dialog. One of you will start with your position about the gun. Pass the paper to your partner for a response. Continue taking turns until you have both finished your arguments.
Example:
Jamal: I want to keep the gun. People are afraid of me when I wear it.
Tito: The gun is a lot of trouble. I think we should get rid of it.

PEER CONFERENCING/REVISING

When you finish the rough draft, ask another pair of students to look at it. You may want to give the students your checklist so they can double check for you and see that you have included all of the information. After reading, they should tell you what they liked best about your persuasive speech, which parts were difficult to understand or needed more information, and ways in which your work could be improved. Reread your persuasive speech considering your critic's comments and make the corrections you think are necessary.

PROOFREADING/EDITING

Do a final proofreading of your persuasive speech, double-checking your grammar, spelling, organization, and the clarity of your ideas.

FINAL DRAFT

Follow your teacher's guidelines for completing the final draft of your paper.

WRITING EVALUATION FORM *Scorpions*
Persuasive Essay

Name _____ Date _____ Class _____

Writing Assignment # _____

Circle One For Each Item:

Composition	excellent	good	fair	poor
Style	excellent	good	fair	poor
Grammar	excellent	good	fair	poor (errors noted)
Spelling	excellent	good	fair	poor (errors noted)
Punctuation	excellent	good	fair	poor (errors noted)
Legibility	excellent	good	fair	poor (errors noted)

Strengths:

Weaknesses:

Comments/Suggestions:

LESSON NINE

Objectives
1. To discuss the main ideas and events in Chapters 10-12
2. To become familiar with the vocabulary for Chapters 13-15
3. To preview the study questions for Chapters 13-15
4. To read Chapters 13-15
5. To record thoughts and ideas in the journal

Activity #1

Divide the class into eight groups. Assign each group one of the study guide questions, and tell the group to prepare a two or three minute skit that answers the study guide question. Since some of these questions deal with the boys fighting and shooting the gun, caution your students to be very careful when preparing and performing the skits.

The students watching the skits should evaluate the performance based on its accuracy according to their study guide answers and the information in the novel.

Activity #2

Put the five vocabulary words for Chapters 13-15 on the board. Ask students to give their ideas of the definitions. Write these on the board. Then work through the worksheet with the students Have them check their definitions with the ones on the worksheet.

Activity #3

Call on students to read the study guide questions aloud to the class.

Activity #4

Give students the rest of the class period to read the chapters. Depending on the needs and abilities of your students, you may want to have them read silently or aloud with a partner.

Activity #5

Give students a few minutes to make journal entries, or remind them to work on their journals outside of class time.

LESSON TEN

<u>Objectives</u>
1. To discuss the main ideas and events in Chapters 13-15
2. To become familiar with the vocabulary for Chapters 16-17
3. To preview the study questions for Chapters 16-17
4. To identify character traits in the main and minor characters
5. To distinguish between homophones *peer, pier*

<u>Activity #1</u>
Distribute copies of the multiple choice quiz/study guide questions for Chapters 13-15. Have students work in pairs to answer the questions. Then check the answers with the whole class.

<u>Activity #2</u>
Give students ten or fifteen minutes to complete the prereading vocabulary worksheet and go over the study guide questions.

<u>Activity #3 Minilesson: Character Development</u>
Explain that an author creates a character, in this case Jamal Hicks, by giving him traits such as physical attributes, thoughts, and feelings. The author develops these traits by telling what the character says, does, and thinks. Writers usually base their characters at least in part on a real person or persons, and then elaborate. A good writer will make the characters believable for the readers.

You may want to use some familiar story or television characters to help students generate a list of character traits. For example, the wolf in the story of *The Three Little Pigs* is very persistent and determined, as shown by his repeated tries to get into the three houses. The largest of the *Three Billy Goats Gruff* is brave or courageous, because he does not let the troll intimidate him.

Explain that *Scorpions* is a "coming-of-age" story where the central character becomes more aware of himself because of events that occur. In this novel, the awareness comes because of Jamal's experience with the Scorpions and the gun.

Have students reread to find evidence of Jamal's character traits. Help them begin filling in one section of the Character Trait Chart (p. 64.) Tell them they should continue to be aware of Jamal's character as they read the last few chapters, and that they will continue the discussion and complete the chart during Lesson Fourteen.

Allow students to work in pairs or individually as they fill in the Character Trait Chart.

<u>Activity #4 (Optional)</u>
You may want to have partners or small groups complete character maps for some of the minor characters, such as Sassy, Mama, Randy, Mack, or Tito.

<u>Activity #5</u>
Call attention to the vocabulary word <u>peer.</u> Tell students that <u>peer</u> and <u>pier</u> (Ch. 6) are homophones, or words that sound alike but have different meanings and spellings. Tell them this clue to help them remember the difference: You <u>peer</u> with your eyes. The words <u>peer</u> and <u>eyes</u> both have two <u>e's</u> in them.

CHARACTER TRAITS CHART
Scorpions

CHARACTER _____

Trait _____	Trait _____	Trait _____	Trait _____
Events That Show It	Events That Show It	Events That Show It	Events That Show It

LESSON ELEVEN

Objectives
1. To discuss the main ideas and events in Chapters 16-17
2. To become familiar with the vocabulary for Chapters 18-20
3. To preview the study guide questions for Chapters 18-20
4. To read Chapters 18-20
5. To participate in a Writing Conference with the teacher

Activity #1
Play a True/False game with students. Divide the class into two teams. Have Team A give an answer to the first question. Team B must determine whether or not the answer is true. If they think the answer is false, they must give the correct answer. Play alternates until all questions have been answered. If you want to keep score, award one point for each correct answer.

Activity #2
Tell students to complete the prereading vocabulary worksheet, preview the study guide questions, and silently read the chapters while you hold individual writing conferences. Remind them that the work will be due at the beginning of the next class period. If they finish the reading assignments, they can work on revising their writing.

Activity #3
Choose a quiet area of the room and hold individual writing conferences.

Activity #4
Assign a due date for the revised versions of the writing assignment.

LESSON TWELVE

Objectives
1. To discuss the main ideas and events in Chapters 18-20
2. To complete a story map

Activity #1
Divide the class into seven groups. Assign a question to each group. Give them a few minutes to prepare an answer. Have a spokesperson from each group give the answer to the question.

Activity #2
Distribute copies of the Story Map (page 66.) Tell students the story map includes all of the elements of a fictional story: characters, setting, problem or conflict, events, and solution or resolution. Review terms as necessary. Help students fill in the details on the story map. Encourage them to reread the text to find details for the map.

Alternate Activity
Instead of using the Story Map to cover the entire story, assign small groups of students to complete a map for each of the reading assignment sections. Then have each group present their information in order according to the story chapters. This will serve as a good review of the main ideas and events in the novel.

Activity #5
Give students a few minutes to make journal entries, or remind them to work on their journals outside of class time.

STORY MAP
Scorpions

CHARACTERS
Main

Minor

SETTING
Time

Place

THEME

POINT OF VIEW

PROBLEM

EVENTS

SOLUTION

LESSON THIRTEEN

Objective
   To practice writing to inform

Activity #1
   Distribute copies of Writing Assignment #3 and go over it in detail with the students. Tell students the assignment will be due during Lesson Twenty. At that time, students will summarize their research in an oral presentation.

Activity #2
   Distribute copies of the Non-Fiction Assignment Sheet and go over it with the students. Tell them to complete the sheet and turn it in with their non-fiction report. It will be used in grading the report.

Activity #3
   Give students the rest of the class period to work on the assignment.

LESSON FOURTEEN

Objective
   To discuss *Scorpions* at the interpretive and critical levels

Activity #1
   Choose the questions from the Extra Writing Assignments/Discussion Questions which seem most appropriate for your students. A class discussion of these questions is most effective if students have been given the opportunity to formulate answers to the questions prior to the discussion. To this end, you may either have all the students formulate answers to all the questions, divide the class into groups and assign one or more questions to each group, or you could assign one question to each student in your class. The option you choose will make a difference in the amount of class time needed for this activity.

Activity #2
   After students have had ample time to formulate answers to the questions, begin your class discussion of the questions and the ideas presented by the questions. Be sure students take notes during the discussion so they have information to study for the unit test.

WRITING ASSIGNMENT #3 *Scorpions*

PROMPT

Scorpions was written in 1988, with a contemporary (modern-day) setting. The author, Walter Dean Myers, uses the story to present some of the problems that children growing up today often face. You will choose a topic related to the story and write an informational report to share with your classmates

PREWRITING

Choose a topic or topics that interest you. Go to the library and find as many sources as you can on the topic. Look for encyclopedias, books, magazine articles, videos, and Internet sources. You may want to interview an expert on the topic of your choice. Some suggestions are: social conditions in modern day Harlem and other urban areas, gangs and gang violence, juvenile delinquency, and handgun regulation.

Think of questions you have about your topic. Write each one on a separate index card. Then read to find the answers, and write them on the cards. Also take notes on interesting and important facts, even if you did not have questions about them. Put each fact on a separate card. Make sure to cite your references. That means to write down the source and the page number for each one.

Arrange your note card in the order you want to use for your paper. Number them, perhaps in the upper right hand corner. Read through them to make sure they make sense in that order. Rearrange as necessary.

DRAFTING

Introduce your topic in the first paragraph. Tell why you chose it, and give a preview of what the rest of the paper will be about. Then write several paragraphs about the topic. Each paragraph should have a main idea and supporting details. Your last paragraph should summarize the information in the report.

PEER CONFERENCE/REVISING

When you finish the rough draft, ask another student to look at it. You may want to give the student your note cards so he/she can double check for you and see that you have included all of the information. After reading, he or she should tell you what he/she liked best about your report, which parts were difficult to understand or needed more information, and ways in which your work could be improved. Reread your report considering your critic's comments and make the corrections you think are necessary.

PROOFREADING/EDITING

Do a final proofreading of your report, double-checking your grammar, spelling, organization, and the clarity of your ideas.

NONFICTION ASSIGNMENT SHEET *Scorpions*

Name _____ Date _____ Class _____

Title of Nonfiction Read _____

Author _____ Publication Date _____

I. **Factual Summary:** Write a short summary of the piece you read.

II. **Vocabulary:**

    1. Which vocabulary words were difficult?

    2. What did you do to help yourself understand the words?

III. **Interpretation:** What was the main point the author wanted you to get from reading his/her work?

IV **Criticism:**

    1. Which points of the piece did you agree with or find easy to believe? Why?

    2. With which points of the piece did you disagree or find difficult to believe? Why?

V. **Personal Response:**
    1. What do you think about this piece?

    2. How does this piece help you better understand the novel *Scorpions?*

EXTRA DISCUSSION QUESTIONS & WRITING ASSIGNMENTS *Scorpions*

Interpretive
1. Describe the neighborhood Jamal lives in. What does it look like? What is the racial mix of the population?
2. Describe the relationship between Jamal and Sassy.
3. How did the principal, Mr. Davidson, and the teacher, Mrs. Rich, treat Jamal? Why did they treat him this way? Ch. 1-3
4. Do you think Jamal wanted to do things correctly in school? Ch. 1-3
5. How did Jamal feel when Mr. Davidson did not notice that he was on time? Ch. 3
6. What kind of student do you think Jamal is? Ch. 1-3
7. Why did Miss Brown tell Jamal to leave instead of asking him to help paint the scenery? Ch. 4
8. Why did Tito like to borrow Jamal's clothes? Ch. 4
9. Why did Tito look embarrassed when Sassy asked him if she were cute? Ch. 5
10. Jamal drew trees when he went to the park. What does this tell about him? Ch. 5
11. Why didn't Mack seem to know the amount of money Randy's lawyer needs? Ch. 5
12. Why did Jamal say he hoped Randy never got out of jail? Ch. 5
13. What did the principal's response to the incident with Oswaldo and Jamal tell you about the principal? Ch. 5
14. What was the significance of the scene at the boat basin? Ch. 6
15. What was the significance of Jamal putting on the Scorpions jacket? How do you think it made Jamal feel? Ch. 7
16. Why are the Scorpions afraid of Mack? Ch. 8
17. Why doesn't Mack take over the Scorpions himself, instead of pressuring Jamal? Ch. 8
18. How did Jamal feel after the fight with Dwayne, when he pulled the gun? Ch. 10
19. How are Jamal's thoughts about having the gun changing? Ch. 10
20. Why did Tito jerk his head away when Jamal said things he did not want to hear? Ch. 11
21. Why did Jamal feel afraid of Dwayne now? Ch. 11
22. Why did Jamal talk about the Scorpions to Dwayne? Ch. 11
23. Why didn't Tito tell Abuela the truth about the gun? Ch. 12
24. Why did Sassy cover for Jamal when the school called? Ch. 13
25. How did Jamal feel when Mr. Gonzalez told him to leave the store? Ch. 13
26. Discuss the irony in the scene where Jamal is drawing a portrait of Tito and they are talking about the gun. Ch. 15
27. What did Jamal's phone conversation with the school secretary say about his character? Ch. 16
28. What did Jamal's phone conversation with Angel say about his character? Ch. 16
29. Why did Jamal tell his mother the pills were vitamins? (Ch. 18)
30. Why did Mack tell Jamal that he (Mack) had killed Angel and wounded Indian? Ch. 19
31. Why did Mrs. Rich take such an interest in Jamal? Ch. 19
32. What was the greatest danger/obstacle that Jamal faced? Why do you think so?

Extra Discussion Questions *Scorpions*

Critical

33. From what point of view is the story written? How does this affect our understanding of the story?
34. What are the main conflicts in the story? Are they resolved? If so, how? If not, why not?
35. What is the setting? How important is the setting to the story? Why?
36. Is the story (plot) believable? Why or why not?
37. How did Jamal change over the course of the novel? Were these changes for the better?
38. Are the characters believable? Why or why not?
39. Walter Dean Myers often used vivid language to describe a scene or event. Give an example of his use of vivid language that you found most effective. Tell why it was effective.
40. What was the overall mood of the story? Give examples to support your answer.
41. How does Walter Dean Myers create suspense?
42. What problem or conflict does the author use to get the story started? How effective is it?
43. Could any of the main events be left out? Which ones? why or why not?
44. could you change the order of the main events and still have the same outcome? If not, how would the outcome change if the order of the events were changed?
45. How would the story have to change to have a different ending?
46. How would the story change if there were a different narrator?
47. Which character do you know the most about? Which character do you know the least about?
48. Were you able to predict the ending? What clues did the author give?
49. Discuss the author's use of language. Is it natural? Do people you know talk the way the characters did?
50. Does the mood of the story change? How does the author show this?
51. What words does the author use to create the atmosphere of the book?
52. Which chapter was most important? Why?
53. Were the descriptions in the book effective? Give some examples.
54. Which senses did the descriptions cause you to use? Give examples of the descriptions using hearing, seeing, touching, smelling, taste.
55. How does the title connect to, or symbolize, the theme of the story?
56. We hear about Randy, but never meet him directly. How effective is this?
57. At which part or parts of the story could Jamal have changed the course of events?

Extra Discussion Questions *Scorpions*

Personal Opinion

58. Mama told Jamal she could not stand it if he were weak. He thought it was hard to be strong. Do you think Jamal was weak or strong? Support your answer with events and quotes from the novel.
59. Do you think Mack would have given the money to Randy for an appeal?
60. What do you think Tito meant about Abuela's "quiet eyes?"
61. How do you think Tito felt when he fired the gun?
62. Why do you think the author waited until Chapter 19 to mention Harlem, the exact setting of the novel,?
63. How do you think Tito and Jamal felt at the end of the story?
64. Did you enjoy reading *Scorpions?* Why or why not?
65. Is *Scorpions* a good title for the book? Why or why not? If not, what title would you suggest?
66. What do you think Jamal will do next? What do you think Tito will do?
67. If you were Jamal, what would you do about joining the Scorpions and/or carrying the gun?
68. Did you have strong feelings while reading this book? If so, what did the author do to cause those feelings? If not, why not?
69. Will you read more books by Walter Dean Myers? Why or why not?
70. Before you read the story, did you think it would be possible to have problems like Jamal's, especially at his age? What do you think after reading the story?
71. Did Jamal's experiences change the way you look at yourself? How?
72. Have you read any other stories similar to *Scorpions?* If so, tell about them.
73. Would you recommend this book to another student? Why or why not?
74. What makes Walter Dean Myers a unique and different author?
75. What questions would you like to ask Walter Dean Myers?
76. What was the funniest part of the story? What was the saddest part? What was the most exciting part?
77. What do you remember most about the story?
78. What picture did the author leave in your mind?
79. What did the book make you think about?

QUOTATIONS *Scorpions*
Discuss the importance of the following quotations.

1. "I don't know," mama said. "He still talking like he ain't got no sense, as far as I'm concerned." Ch. 1
2. "That's what brothers do," said Tito. Ch. 4
3. "You can say a lie faster than you can say the truth, girl." Ch. 4, Jamal
4. "If she say one word about him being in jail, I'm leaving your house and we never going to be friends again." Ch. 4, Jamal
5. "The Scorpions ain't just turning over their gang to me." Ch. 5, Jamal
6. "Jamal, I don't like that guy. he act like he using crack or something." Ch. 5, Tito
7. "One day," --Mama's eyes looked far away--"I was walking downtown with Randy in my arms. I was waiting for a light to change when this white lady stopped and looked at him. I looked at her and she was smiling and I smiled back at her, and that was the best feeling in the whole world. You got a baby and you hope so much for it . . . . " Ch. 5
8. "Lord Jesus!" Mama said. "Lord Jesus, what is this family coming to?" Ch. 5
9. "I'm not going to give you a warning because I don't think it's going to do any good," Mr. Davidson said to Jamal. "So you just go on and do what you want to do. sooner or later you're going to do something that's going to let me put you out of the school. You know that and I know that. Go on now to your classroom." Ch. 6
10. "We gonna have to settle this mess," Dwayne said when they reached math. "You gonna punk out?"
    "I'll be there," Jamal said. "Just bring your butt so I can kick it again. " Ch. 7
11. "I see he got the part, but I don't know if he got the heart," Indian said. Ch. 8
12. "Well, that's better. I know you don't want me to have to take my belt off and straighten you out." Ch. 9, Jevon Hicks
13. "I'm the leader of the Scorpions." Jamal, Ch. 10
14. "Go on, shoot it." Jamal, Ch. 11

15. "I was thinking about going to the police and telling them you got a gun," Dwayne said. Ch. 11

16. "Tito, sometimes we women got to be harder on you young boys than we want to be. You know that and I know that. Me and your grandmother, we try our best, but God knows it's hard. We say things we don't mean because to say the things we mean is just too hurtin'. You be all right, 'cause that woman loves you as much as she loves life." Ch. 12
17. "That gun is too much trouble." Ch. 12, Tito
18. "Pictures! Little boys draw pictures. This is what I want Tito to do. Draw pictures like a little boy." Ch. 13, Abuela
19. "Your brother's gone, man. You next." Ch. 13, Angel

Quotations *Scorpions*

20. He didn't want to think about anything happening to the family. It seemed like they never made things happen to anybody else, or even for themselves. Things happened to his family, the same way things happened to him. Ch. 14

21. "Sometimes the herbs we take are bitter, sister, but we got to take them anyway. The important thing here is that, as much as your heart is with your boy in the hospital, you got to hold your family here together, too. We can't let the bad mess up the good." Ch. 13

22. "I can't stand to have you weak, Jamal," Mama said. "I can't stand it now." Ch. 14
23. "They look like they thrown-away people," Tito said. "That makes me scared, because I don't want to be no thrown-away guy." Ch. 15
24. "You going to feel good when you're not in the Scorpions anymore," (Tito) said. "I'll be glad when things get back to normal." Ch. 16
25. "Lord, when am I going to learn that my problems don't belong to nobody but me?" Mama started rocking back and forth. "Lord, when am I going to *learn?*"
26. Jamal wondered if there would ever be a time in his life when he didn't have to worry about somebody beating him up, or being in a fight with someone. Ch. 17

27. "We all born with sense," Mama said. "Lord knows what happens to it along the way." Ch. 18

28. "They layin' low," Mack said. "You waste a couple of guys, and they know you mean what you say." Ch. 19

LESSON FIFTEEN

Objectives
    1. To extend the story by means of a project
    2. To work cooperatively in a group

Activity #1
    Allow students to choose one of the following projects. Give them the class period to complete it. If students need more time, you can assign the project as homework or add another day onto the unit plan.

PROJECT IDEAS

1. Draw a book jacket that summarizes the story.
2. Write a critique of the book.
3. Make a timeline showing the important events from the story.
4. Make a diorama showing one of the scenes from the book.
5. Make a drawing showing the Scorpions' shield.
6. Write a radio or television commercial to advertise the book.
7. Design a poster to advertise the book.
8. Write a different ending to the story.
9. Make a comic book version of the story to share with younger readers.
10. Make a mobile showing the main character, secondary characters and setting.
11. Make a collage based on scenes from the book.
12. Outline the events that might happen in a sequel.
13. Make a scrapbook about the story. Draw or cut out pictures to represent the important events. Collect items that the main characters might have had (such as drawing paper and pencils for Jamal) and put them in the scrapbook.
14. Write a riddle to describe one of the characters. Put the name of the character on the back of the riddle.
15. Write an acrostic poem using the name of one of the characters. Put the name of the character down the left side of the paper. Next to each letter in the name, write a word or phrase to describe the person. Example: J= jumpy in school; A= artistic, etc. Decorate the acrostic poem by making the letters in the character's name a different size or style.
16. Dramatize one of the incidents in the story. Write dialog for the characters.
17. Design and produce a talk show. Choose one of the story incidents as the topic. The host will interview the various characters. (Students should make up the questions they want the host to ask the characters.)

LESSON SIXTEEN

Objectives
1. To use library resources for research
2. To complete the writing assignment and/or project

Activity #1
Take students to the library. Assist as necessary in showing them how to use the print and on-line resources to find information about their topics.

Activity #2
If you don't go to the library, give students time in the classroom to work on their writing assignments and/or projects.

LESSON SEVENTEEN

Objective
To review all of the vocabulary work done in this unit

Activities
Choose one or more of the following activities to use for reviewing the vocabulary words.

1. Divide your class into two teams and have an old-fashioned spelling or definition bee.

2. Give individuals or groups of students a Vocabulary Word Search Puzzle. The person (group) to find all of the vocabulary words in the puzzle first wins.

3. Give students a Vocabulary Word Search Puzzle without the word list. The person or group to find the most vocabulary words in the puzzle wins.

4. Put a Vocabulary Crossword Puzzle onto a transparency on the overhead projector and do the puzzle together as a class.

5. Give students a Vocabulary Matching Worksheet to do.

6. Use words from the word jumble page and have students spell them correctly.

7. Have students write a story in which they correctly use as many vocabulary words as possible. Have students read their compositions orally. Post the most original compositions on your bulletin board.

8. Have students work in teams and play charades with the vocabulary words.

   Vocabulary Review Activities Continued *Scorpions*

9. Select a word of the day and encourage students to use it correctly in their writing and speaking vocabulary.

10. Have a contest to see which students can find the most vocabulary words used in other sources. You may want to have a bulletin board available so the students can write down their word, the sentence it was used in, and the source.

11. Assign a word to each student, or let them choose a word. Have them look up the origin of the word, the part of speech, definition, a synonym, and an antonym. Then have them write a sentence using the word. Have students present their information orally to the class, or have them design a word map on paper and display the papers.

LESSON EIGHTEEN

Objective
To review the main ideas presented in *Scorpions*

Activity #1
Choose one of the review games/activities included in the packet and spend your class period as outlined there.

Activity #2
Remind students of the date for the Unit Test. Stress the review of the Study Guides and their class notes as a last minute, brush-up review for homework.

UNIT REVIEW GAMES / ACTIVITIES

1. Ask the class to make up a unit test for *Scorpions*. The test should have 4 sections: multiple choice, true/false, short answer and essay. Students may use 1/2 period to make the test, including a separate answer sheet, and then swap papers and use the other 1/2 class period to take a test a classmate has devised. (open book)

2. Take 1/2 period for students to make up true and false questions (including the answers). Collect the papers and divide the class into two teams. Draw a big tic-tac-toe board on the chalk board. Make one team X and one team O. Ask questions to each side, giving each student one turn. If the question is answered correctly, that student's team's letter (X or O) is placed in the box. If the answer is incorrect, no mark is placed in the box. The object is to get three marks in a row like tic-tac-toe. You may want to keep track of the number of games won for each team.

3. Take 1/2 period for students to make up questions (true/false and short answer). Collect the questions. Divide the class into two teams. You'll alternate asking questions to individual members of teams A & B (like in a spelling bee). The question keeps going from A to B until it is correctly answered, then a new question is asked. A correct answer does not allow the team to get another question. Correct answers are +2 points; incorrect answers are -1 point.

4. Allow students time to quiz each other (in pairs) from their study guides and class notes.

5. Give students a *Scorpions* crossword puzzle to complete.

Unit Review Activities Continued *Scorpions*

6. Divide your class into two teams. Use the crossword words with their letters jumbled as a word list. Student 1 from Team A faces off against Student 1 from Team B. You write the first jumbled word on the board. The first student (1A or 1B) to unscramble the word wins the chance for his/her team to score points. If 1A wins the jumble, go to student 2A and give him/her a clue. He/she must give you the correct word which matches that clue. If he/she does, Team A scores a point, and you give student 3A a clue for which you expect another correct response. Continue giving Team A clues until some team member makes an incorrect response. An incorrect response sends the game back to the jumbled-word face off, this time with students 2A and 2B. Instead of repeating giving clues to the first few students of each team, continue with the student after the one who gave the last incorrect response on the team.

7. Take on the persona of "The Answer Person." Allow students to ask any question about the book. Answer the questions, or tell students where to look in the book to find the answer.

8. Students may enjoy playing charades with events from the story. Select a student to start. Give him/her a card with a scene or event from the story. Allow the players to use their books to find the scene being described. The first person to guess each charade performs the next one.

9. Play a categories-type quiz game. Make an overhead transparency of the categories form. Divide the class into teams of three or four players each. Have each team Choose a recorder and a banker. Choose a team to go first. That team will choose a category and point amount. Ask the question to the entire class.(Use the Study Guide Quiz and Vocabulary questions.) Give the teams one minute to discuss the answer and write it down. Walk around the room and check the answers. Each team that answers correctly receives the points. (Incorrect answers are not penalized; they just don't receive any points). Cross out that square on the playing board. Play continues until all squares have been used. The winning team is the one with the most points. You can assign bonus points to any square or squares you choose.

10. Have individual students draw scenes from the book. Display the scenes and have the rest of the class look in their books to find the chapter or section that is being depicted. The first student to find the correct scene then displays his or her picture. When the game is over, collect the pictures and put them in a binder for students to look at during their free time.

NOTE: If students do not need the extra review, omit this lesson and go on to the test.

QUIZ GAME *Scorpions*

Chapters 1-3 & 4-5	Chapters 6-7 & 8-9	Chapters 10-12 & 13-15	Chapters 16-17 & 18-20	Vocabulary
100	100	100	100	100
200	200	200	200	200
300	300	300	300	300
400	400	400	400	400
500	500	500	500	500

LESSON NINETEEN

Objective
To test the students' understanding of the main ideas and themes in *Scorpions*

Activity #1
Distribute the *Scorpions* Unit Tests. Go over the instructions in detail and allow the students the entire class period to complete the exam.

Activity #2
Collect all test papers and assigned books prior to the end of the class period.

LESSON TWENTY

Objectives
1. To widen the breadth of students' knowledge about the topics discussed or touched upon in *Scorpions*
2. To check students' non-fiction assignments

Activity
Ask each student to give a brief oral report about the nonfiction work he/she read for the nonfiction assignment. Your criteria for evaluating this report will vary depending on the level of your students. You may wish for students to give a complete report without using notes of any kind, or you may want students to read directly from a written report, or you may want to do something in between these two extremes. Just make students aware of your criteria in ample time for them to prepare their reports.

Start with one student's report. After that, ask if anyone else in the class has read on a topic related to the first student's report. If no one has, choose another student at random. After each report, be sure to ask if anyone has a report related to the one just completed. That will help keep a continuity during the discussion of the reports.

UNIT TESTS

NOTES ABOUT THE UNIT TESTS IN THIS UNIT:

There are 5 different unit tests which follow.

There are two short answer tests which are based primarily on facts from the novel. The answer key for short answer unit test 1 follows the student test. The answer key for short answer test 2 follows the student short answer unit test 2.

There is one advanced short answer unit test. It is based on the extra discussion questions. Use the matching key for short answer unit test 2 to check the matching section of the advanced short answer unit test. There is no key for the short answer questions. The answers will be based on the discussions you have had during class.

There are two multiple choice unit tests. Following the two unit tests, you will find an answer sheet on which students should mark their answers. The same answer sheet should be used for both tests; however, students' answers will be different for each test. Following the students' answer sheet for the multiple choice tests you will find your answer keys.

The short answer tests have a vocabulary section. You should choose 10 of the vocabulary words from this unit, read them orally and have the students write them down. Then, either have students write a definition or use the words in sentences. The second part of the vocabulary test is matching.

SHORT ANSWER UNIT TEST 1 *Scorpions*

I. Matching/ Identify

1. Jamal
2. Tito
3. Randy
4. Mack
5. Mama
6. Sassy
7. Jevon
8. Angel
9. Indian
10. Abuela

A. bragged about a shooting he did not commit
B. his comments made Jamal feel bad
C. thought the gun was trouble
D. took her grandson back to Puerto Rico
E. wanted to earn money for his brother's appeal
F. was wounded during the fight in the park
G. working and trying to keep the family together
H. killed during the fight in the park
I. in prison for his part in a robbery
J. knew about the gun but did not tell

II. Short Answer

1. What were some of the things that made Jamal feel small inside?

2. How did Mack suggest that Jamal get the money for Randy?

Short Answer Unit Test 1 *Scorpions*

3. Answer the following questions to describe Jamal's school life. What kind of difficulties did Jamal have in school. How did Mr. Davisdon treat him? Which teachers did he like? Why did Mr. Davidson want to see Mrs. Hicks? What did the principal and the school nurse do to try and help him?

4. What happened when Jamal and Tito met Indian and Angel in the park?

5. Discuss the meaning and importance of the following passage from the novel: Jamal wondered if there would ever be a time in his life when he didn't have to worry about somebody beating him up, or being in a fight with someone.

Short Answer Unit Test 1 *Scorpions*

III. Fill-in-the-Blank

Directions: Use a word or phrase to complete each sentence about the story.

1. Jamal was having trouble in school with a boy named _____.

2. The two boys fought in the _____.

3. Then Jamal pulled out _____. This ended the fight.

4. When Jamal left school after the fight he was _____.

5. The Scorpions did not want _____ working with them because he would be tried and sentenced as an adult if he got caught again.

6. The Scorpions only wanted _____ boys who would not be in danger of doing time, or testifying against them.

7. Tito told his grandmother about the gun, but said he had been _____. She got a lawyer and they wen to the police.

8. The police charged Tito with being a _____.

9. The police said if Tito _____ he would not be in trouble.

10. Jamal gave Tito the _____ .

IV. Essay

What are the main conflicts in the story? Are they resolved? If so, how? If not, why not?

Short Answer Unit Test 1 *Scorpions*

IV. Vocabulary
Listen to the vocabulary words and spell them. After you have spelled all the words, go back and write down the definitions.

WORD   **DEFINITION**

1. _____   _____

2. _____   _____

3. _____   _____

4. _____   _____

5. _____   _____

6. _____   _____

7. _____   _____

8. _____   _____

9. _____   _____

10. _____   _____

Vocabulary Part 2   Matching.

1. subway   A. low and broad
2. squat   B. with silent resentment
3. episode   C. a pleasant odor
4. bannister   D. a building's small porch or staircase
5. gravelly   E. harmful waste matter
6. aroma   F. sounding harsh or rasping
7. pollution   G. government funded housing for the poor
8. projects   H. one part of a serial story or sow
9. sullenly   I. an underground, electric railway
10. stoop   J. a handrail

ANSWER KEY SHORT ANSWER UNIT TEST 1 *Scorpions*

I. <u>Matching/ Identify</u>

E	1.	Jamal	A.	bragged about a shooting he did not commit
C	2.	Tito	B.	his comments made Jamal feel bad
I	3.	Randy	C.	thought the gun was trouble
A	4.	Mack	D.	took her grandson back to Puerto Rico
G	5.	Mama	E.	wanted to earn money for his brother's appeal
J	6.	Sassy	F.	was wounded during the fight in the park
B	7.	Jevon	G.	working and trying to keep the family together
H	8.	Angel	H.	killed during the fight in the park
F	9.	Indian	I.	in prison for his part in a robbery
D	10.	Abuela	J.	knew about the gun but did not tell

1. What were some of the things that made Jamal feel small inside?
   Dwayne, the man at the furniture store, teachers who called attention to him when he made a mistake or forgot his homework, big kids who laughed at him all made Jamal feel small.

2. How did Mack suggest that Jamal get the money for Randy?
   Mack said Jamal should take over the Scorpions. Then they could make money by carrying for the Spanish guys.

3. Answer the following questions to describe Jamal's school life. What kind of difficulties did Jamal have in school. How did Mr. Davisdon treat him? Which teachers did he like? Why did Mr. Davidson want to see Mrs. Hicks? What did the principal and the school nurse do to try and help him?
   Jamal had a hard time in school. He had trouble paying attention, and had low grades. Another student, Dwayne, was picking fights. Jamal liked Mrs. Roberts, the school nurse, because she gave out peppermints. Miss Brown was is favorite teacher. Mr. Davidson wanted to talk to Mrs. Hicks about sending Jamal to a special school for problem students. he and Mrs. Roberts had Jamal take a form home to his mother. The form gave the school nurse permission to give Jamal some medicine to calm him down. She said he was the most hyperactive child she had ever seen.

4. What happened when Jamal and Tito met Indian and Angel in the park?
   Jamal told Indian and Angel that Randy said Indian was to be the leader. He also he was giving up the Scorpions' colors. Angel said he could not give up the colors unless the leader agreed. Then Angel and Indian started beating on Jamal. Angel pulled out a knife. Tito, who had been holding the gun, fired it. Angel fell to the ground and Indian crawled away. Tito and Jamal ran out of the park.

5. Discuss the meaning and importance of the following passage from the novel: Jamal wondered if there would ever be a time in his life when he didn't have to worry about somebody beating him up, or being in a fight with someone.

> This quote is from Chapter 17. Jamal was waiting outside of Tito's building for him to sneak out. A wino was giving Jamal his opinion about Puerto Ricans. He suggested that having a Puerto Rican friend was not a good idea, because they were not trustworthy. Jamal and Tito were preparing to meet Indian and Blood in the park so that Jamal could quit the Scorpions.

III. Fill-in-the-Blank
1. Jamal was having trouble in school with a boy named **_Dwayne_**.
2. The two boys fought in the **_storeroom at school_**.
3. Then Jamal pulled out **_the gun_**. This ended the fight.
4. When Jamal left school after the fight he was **_crying_**.
5. The Scorpions did not want **_Mack_** working with them because he would be tried and sentenced as an adult if he got caught again.
6. The Scorpions only wanted **_younger_** boys who would not be in danger of doing time, or testifying against them.
7. Tito told his grandmother about the gun, but said he had been **_alone_**. She got a lawyer and they wen to the police.
8. The police charged Tito with being a **_juvenile delinquent_**.
9. The police said if Tito **_went back to Puerto Rico_** he would not be in trouble.
10. Jamal gave Tito the **_portrait he had made earlier_**.

IV. *Essay*
Answers will vary depending on the class discussions.

V. Vocabulary Part I Choose ten words to dictate for this section of the test.

Vocabulary Part 2

I	1.	subway	A.	low and broad
A	2.	squat	B.	with silent resentment
H	3.	episode	C.	a pleasant odor
J	4.	bannister	D.	a building's small porch or staircase
F	5.	gravelly	E.	harmful waste matter
C	6.	aroma	F.	sounding harsh or rasping
E	7.	pollution	G.	government funded housing for the poor
G	8.	projects	H.	one part of a serial story or sow
B	9.	sullenly	I.	an underground, electric railway
D	10.	stoop	J.	a handrail

SHORT ANSWER UNIT TEST 2 *Scorpions*

I. <u>Matching/ Identify</u>

1.	Mr. Stanton	A.	Jamal told him to be the new gang leader
2.	Dwayne	B.	thought Jamal needed a special school
3.	Tito	C.	told her younger son she needed him to be strong
4.	Blood	D.	liked to wear Jamal's clothes
5.	Angel	E.	told on Randy to reduce his own sentence
6.	Indian	F.	was shot and killed during the fight
7.	Mack	G.	would not loan Mama the money for an appeal
8.	Abuela	H.	first to notice Jamal's gun
9.	Mrs. Hicks	I.	picked fights in school with Jamal
10.	Mr. Davidson	J.	put her grandson out when she found the gun

II. <u>Short Answer</u>

1. Describe the situation between Jamal and Dwayne. Include the incidents that lead up to the fight, the fight, and what happened afterwards.

2. Summarize Jamal's experience with his job. Tell about the kind of job, where it was, and what happened while Jamal was working.

Short Answer Unit Test 2 *Scorpions*

3. Who gave the gun to Jamal, and why? How did Tito feel about the gun?

4. What was Randy's problem? How were Mama, Jamal, and Mack trying to help? How did the Scorpions feel about helping?

5. Explain the importance of the following quotation. Tell who said it, and to whom the speaker was talking. "You waste a couple of guys, and they know you mean what you say."

Short Answer Unit Test 2 *Scorpions*

III. Fill-in-the-Blanks   Directions: Use a word or phrase to complete each sentence about the story.

1. Jamal made a phone call to _____.

2. He told Angel that Randy had told his mother that _____ should be the leader.

3. Angel said they wanted to meet with Jamal in Marcus Garvey Park so that _____
   _____ _____.

4. Jamal told Tito that if Indian started to beat him up, he would _____
   _____ .

5. When they all met in the park, Jamal repeated what he had said on the phone. He also said he was
   _____ .

6. Angel said Jamal could not do that unless _____ .

7. Then Angel and Indian started _____ .

8. Angel pulled out _____ .

9. _____ , who had been holding the gun, fired it.

10. _____ fell to the ground, dead, and _____ crawled away.

IV. Essay
     How did Jamal change from the beginning to the end of the novel? Were these changes for the better? What outside circumstances influenced these changes?

Short Answer Unit Test 2 *Scorpions*

V. Vocabulary

Directions: Listen to the vocabulary words and spell them. After you have spelled all the words, go back and write down the definitions.

WORD	**DEFINITION**
1. _____	_____
2. _____	_____
3. _____	_____
4. _____	_____
5. _____	_____
6. _____	_____
7. _____	_____
8. _____	_____
9. _____	_____
10. _____	_____

Vocabulary Part 2 Matching.

1. parole
2. stocky
3. slick
4. projects
5. bobbing
6. pier
7. glanced
8. vaguely
9. beckoned
10. peer

A. gazed briefly
B. shrewd
C. government funded housing for the poor
D. not clearly expressed
E. a platform over the water
F. made a signaling gesture
G. solidly built; sturdy
H. moving up and down
I. to look or search
J. supervised freedom from prison

ANSWER KEY SHORT ANSWER UNIT TEST 2 *Scorpions*

I. <u>Matching/ Identify</u>

G	1.	Mr. Stanton	A.	Jamal told him to be the new gang leader
I	2.	Dwayne	B.	thought Jamal needed a special school
D	3.	Tito	C.	told her younger son she needed him to be strong
H	4.	Blood	D.	liked to wear Jamal's clothes
F	5.	Angel	E.	told on Randy to reduce his own sentence
A	6.	Indian	F.	was shot and killed during the fight
E	7.	Mack	G.	would not loan Mama the money for an appeal
J	8.	Abuela	H.	first to notice Jamal's gun
C	9.	Mrs. Hicks	I.	picked fights in school with Jamal
B	10.	Mr. Davidson	J.	put her grandson out when she found the gun

II. <u>Short Answer</u>

1. Describe the situation between Jamal and Dwayne. Include the incidents that lead up to the fight, the fight, and what happened afterwards.

    Dwayne insulted Jamal by criticizing his sneakers. Dwayne also said Jamal looked like a frog. Jamal threatened to put one of the sneakers upside Dwayne's head.

    They fought in the storeroom at school. They both landed some punches, and Jamal ripped Dwayne's shirt. Then Jamal pulled out the gun. He noticed Dwayne's fear, and Dwayne begged him not to shoot. Then Jamal put the gun back in the bag, and left the school building.

    The next day Dwayne said he was thinking of telling the police about Jamal's gun. Jamal asked him if he wanted to mess with the Scorpions.

    The following Monday there was a meeting with Mr.. Davidson, Jamal, Dwayne, and his mother. Dwayne told them all about the gun. Mrs. Parsons wanted Mr. Davidson to call the police, but he said he could not do that unless he had proof that Jamal had a gun. Jamal denied having the gun. Mrs. Parsons said she was going to see a lawyer, and she left. Mr. Davidson said Jamal would have to sit in the lunchroom every day until his mother came to school.

2. Summarize Jamal's experience with his job. Tell about the kind of job, where it was, and what happened while Jamal was working.

    He worked in the bodega for Mr. Gonzalez. He stocked the shelves and carried groceries for customers.

    Right after the meeting with Dwayne and Mr. Davidson, Jamal went to work. Indian and Angel were there waiting for him. Indian took some candy bars, then knocked over the dominoes on the table. Jamal thought he looked high. After they left, Mr. Gonzalez told Jamal to leave.

3. Who gave the gun to Jamal, and why? How did Jamal and Tito feel about the gun?

    Mack gave the gun to Jamal, because Mack wanted Jamal to be the new leader of the Scorpions. Tito did not like having the gun around, because he thought it was a lot of trouble. He wanted to get rid of it. Jamal was not sure how he felt. Most of the time he did not like having the gun, but during the fight with Dwayne and the first meeting with the Scorpions, having the gun made him feel less afraid.

4. What was Randy's problem? How were Mama, Jamal, and Mack trying to help? How did the Scorpions feel about helping?

    Randy was in prison for shooting someone during a robbery. He wanted his family and the Scorpions to raise two thousand dollars to get a new appeal. Mama was working extra hours. She also asked her boss, Mr. Stanton, for a loan, but he refused. Mack wanted Jamal to take over the Scorpions, then have them run drugs for the Spanish gang to get the money. Jamal got a job at a bodega, but lost it when Indian and Blood made trouble in the store.

5. Explain the importance of the following quotation. Tell who said it, and to whom the speaker was talking. "You waste a couple of guys, and they know you mean what you say."

    Mack was talking to Jamal the day after the fight in the park when Angel was killed. He was bragging that he had killed Angel and wounded Indian.

III. Fill-in-the-Blanks

1. Jamal made a phone call to ***Indian/the Scorpions.***
2. He told Angel that Randy had told his mother that ***Indian*** should be the leader.
3. Angel said they wanted to meet with Jamal in Marcus Garvey Park so that ***Jamal could tell the same thing to all of the Scorpions.***
4. Jamal told Tito that if Indian started to beat him up, he would ***take it, then walk away, go home, wash up, and laugh.***
5. When they all met in the park, Jamal repeated what he had said on the phone. He also said he was ***giving up the Scorpions' colors.***
6. Angel said Jamal could not do that unless ***the leader agreed***.
7. Then Angel and Indian started ***beating on Jamal***.
8. Angel pulled out ***a knife***.
9. ***Tito***, who had been holding the gun, fired it.
10. ***Angel*** fell to the ground, dead, and ***Indian*** crawled away.

IV. Essay

How did Jamal change from the beginning to the end of the novel? Were these changes for the better? What outside circumstances influenced these changes?

Answers will vary, depending on classroom discussions.

V. <u>Vocabulary</u> Choose ten of the vocabulary words to dictate for this portion of the test.

<u>Vocabulary Part 2</u>

J	1.	parole	A.	gazed briefly
G	2.	stocky	B.	shrewd
B	3.	slick	C.	government funded housing for the poor
C	4.	projects	D.	not clearly expressed
H	5.	bobbing	E.	a platform over the water
E	6.	pier	F.	made a signaling gesture
A	7.	glanced	G.	solidly built; sturdy
D	8.	vaguely	H.	moving up and down
F	9.	beckoned	I.	to look or search
I	10.	peer	J.	supervised freedom from prison

ADVANCED SHORT ANSWER TEST *Scorpions*

I. <u>Matching/ Identify</u>

1. Mr. Stanton
2. Dwayne
3. Tito
4. Blood
5. Angel
6. Indian
7. Mack
8. Abuela
9. Mrs. Hicks
10. Mr. Davidson

A. Jamal told him to be the new gang leader
B. thought Jamal needed a special school
C. told her younger son she needed him to be strong
D. liked to wear Jamal's clothes
E. told on Randy to reduce his own sentence
F. was shot and killed during the fight
G. would not loan Mama the money for an appeal
H. first to notice Jamal's gun
I. picked fights in school with Jamal
J. put her grandson out when she found the gun

II. <u>Short Answer</u>
1. What are the main conflicts in the story? Are they resolved? If so, how? If not, way not?

2. How does Jamal change from the beginning to the end of the novel? Which of these changes are for the better? Which are not? What outside forces or events influenced the changes in Jamal?

Advanced Short Answer Test *Scorpions*

3. Discuss the irony in the scene where Jamal is drawing a portrait of Tito and they are talking about the gun.

4. Mama told Jamal she could not stand it if he were weak. He thought it was hard to be strong. Do you think Jamal was weak or strong? Support your answer with events and quotes from the story.

5. What was the greatest danger/obstacle Jamal faced? Why do you think so?

Advanced Short Answer Unit Test *Scorpions*

III. Quotations

Directions: Discuss the importance of the following quotations. Include who said the quote, and to whom they were speaking.

1. "I'm not going to give you a warning because I don't think it's going to do any good. So you just go on and do what you want to do. Sooner or later you're going to do something that's going to let me put you out of the school. You know that and I know that. Go on now to your classroom."

2. "Your brother's gone, man. You next."

3. "That's what brothers do."

4. "Go on, shoot it."

5. "They layin' low. You waste a couple of guys, and they know you mean what you say."

Advanced Short Answer Test *Scorpions*

IV. Vocabulary

Listen to the words and write them down. After you have written down all of the words, write a paragraph in which you use all of the words. The paragraph must in some way relate to *Scorpions*.

1.   6.
2.   7.
3.   8.
4.   9.
5.   10.

MULTIPLE CHOICE UNIT TEST 1 *Scorpions*

I. Matching/ Identify

1. Jamal
2. Tito
3. Randy
4. Mack
5. Mama
6. Sassy
7. Jevon
8. Angel
9. Indian
10. Abuela

A. bragged about a shooting he did not commit
B. his comments made Jamal feel bad
C. thought the gun was trouble
D. took her grandson back to Puerto Rico
E. wanted to earn money for his brother's appeal
F. was wounded during the fight in the park
G. working and trying to keep the family together
H. killed during the fight in the park
I. in prison for his part in a robbery
J. knew about the gun but did not tell

II. Multiple Choice Directions: Circle the letter in front of the sentence that answers the question.

1. Which statement about the characters is **false**?
   A. Jamal Hicks is a seventh grade boy.
   B. Randy is in jail for robbing a bank.
   C. Sassy is in the third grade.
   D. Mrs. Hicks works and tries to take care of the family.

2. Which sentence about Mack is **true**?
   A. Mrs. Hicks liked him.
   B. Randy made him the temporary leader of the Scorpions.
   C. He had killed three members of another gang, but had not been caught.
   D. He had been in a juvenile home for breaking a man's arm.

3. How did Jamal feel about Randy?
   A. Jamal liked the cool way Randy looked when he heard the guilty verdict.
   B. He thought his big brother was perfect.
   C. He was mad at Randy because of the way Mama cried about his prison sentence.
   D. Jamal did not like the tough-guy act that Randy always put on.

4. What did Jamal think Randy was doing to Mama?
   A. He was making her tired.
   B. He was stealing her money.
   C. He was lying to her.
   D. He was beating her.

Multiple Choice Unit Test 1 *Scorpions*

5. Tito and Jamal talked about something they both wanted to own. What was it?
    A. They both wanted to buy big, beautiful houses for their families.
    B. They both wanted to own boats.
    C. They both wanted to own guns.
    D. They both wanted to own fast sports cars.

6. True or False: Tito thought he and Jamal could get the Scorpions to do some good.
    A. True
    B. False

7. True or False: Dwayne went right to the police and told them about the gun.
    A. True
    B. False

8. What was Jamal's phone message to Indian?
    A. Jamal said he would take Indian out if he opposed having Jamal be the leader.
    B. He said that Randy had told his mother that Indian should be the leader, and the Scorpions should get the money for his appeal.
    C. Jamal said he was too young to be a Scorpion. If they would leave him alone, he would leave them alone.
    D. Jamal said he was giving the gun back to Mack, and that Mack should be the leader.

9. Which event did **not** happened when Jamal and Tito met Indian and Angel in the park?
    A. Jamal told Indian and Angel that Randy said Indian was to be the leader.
    B. Angel pulled out a knife.
    C. Angel and Indian started beating on Jamal.
    D. Indian told Jamal he was expelled from the Scorpions.

10. What happened to Tito?
    A. He was sent to reform school for three years.
    B. Tito and his grandmother returned to Puerto Rico.
    C. Nothing. The lawyer said it was self defense and there were no charges.
    D. He ran away and was never heard from again.

Multiple Choice Unit Test 1 *Scorpions*

III. Quotations

Directions: Identify the speaker of each quotation. Put the letter of the speaker on the line after the quotation.

A. Angel   B. Mama   C. Indian   D. Tito   E. Reverend Biggs

F. Abuela   G. Mack   H. Dwayne   I. Jevon   J. Jamal

___ 1. "I see he got the part, but I don't know if he got the heart."

___ 2. "Well, that's better. I know you don't want me to have to take my belt off and straighten you out."

___ 3. "Go on. Shoot it."

___ 4. "We gonna have to settle this mess. You gonna punk out?"

___ 5. "That's what brothers do.

___ 6. "Pictures! Little boys draw pictures. This is what I want Tito to do. Draw pictures like a little boy."

___ 7. "Sometimes the herbs we take are bitter, sister, but we got to take them anyway. The important thing here is that, as much as your heart is with your boy in the hospital, you got to hold your family here together, too. We can't let the bad mess up the good."

___ 8. "Lord, when am I going to learn that my problems don't belong to nobody but me? Lord, when am I going to *learn?*"

___ 9. "They layin' low. You waste a couple of guys, and they know you mean what you say."

___ 10. "Your brother's gone, man. You next."

Extra Credit: Draw a picture to go with one of the quotations. Write three or four sentences describing your illustration. Identify the characters, setting, and event that you have drawn.

Multiple Choice Unit Test 1 *Scorpions*

Vocabulary Part 1   Directions: Place the letter of the matching definition on the blank line.

1. subway
2. squat
3. episode
4. bannister
5. gravelly
6. aroma
7. pollution
8. projects
9. sullenly
10. stoop

A. low and broad
B. with silent resentment
C. a pleasant odor
D. a building's small porch or staircase
E. harmful waste matter
F. sounding harsh or rasping
G. government funded housing for the poor
H. one part of a serial story or sow
I. an underground, electric railway
J. a handrail

Vocabulary Part 2   Directions: Circle the letter next to the word that matches the definition.

11. **persisted; stayed**
    A. clenched
    B. glisten
    C. lingered
    D. glanced

12. **holding without ownership**
    A. tenements
    B. strut
    C. possession
    D. beckoned

13. **bent or sagged downward**
    A. glanced
    B. stammered
    C. clenched
    D. drooped

14. **someone who disobeys the law**
    A. shield
    B. bannister
    C. musty
    D. delinquent

15. **rapidly; quickly**
    A. sullenly
    B. hastily
    C. glisten
    D. droopy

16. **for or about young people or children**
    A. delinquent
    B. squat
    C. slick
    D. juvenile

17. **images**
    A. peer
    B. reflections
    C. slits
    D. projects

18. **small containers with stoppers**
    A. vials
    B. slits
    C. reflections
    D. tenements

19. **to look or search**
    A. pier
    B. peer
    C. beckoned
    D. stoop

20. **tripped**
    A. stumbled
    B. stammered
    C. glanced
    D. clenched

MULTIPLE CHOICE UNIT TEST 2 *Scorpions*

I. <u>Matching/ Identify</u>

1. Mr. Stanton
2. Dwayne
3. Tito
4. Blood
5. Angel
6. Indian
7. Mack
8. Abuela
9. Mrs. Hicks
10. Mr. Davidson

A. Jamal told him to be the new gang leader
B. thought Jamal needed a special school
C. told her younger son she needed him to be strong
D. liked to wear Jamal's clothes
E. told on Randy to reduce his own sentence
F. was shot and killed during the fight
G. would not loan Mama the money for an appeal
H. first to notice Jamal's gun
I. picked fights in school with Jamal
J. put her grandson out when she found the gun

II. <u>Multiple Choice</u>

1. What did Randy want Jamal to do?
    A. Randy wanted Jamal to be good and take care of their mother.
    B. Randy wanted Jamal to get a job and save up the money for an appeal.
    C. Randy wanted Jamal to start a new gang to fight the Scorpions.
    D. Randy wanted Jamal to go and see Mack.

2. What did Jamal do well?
    A. He was an excellent singer.
    B. He was very good at telling jokes.
    C. He was good at drawing and painting.
    D. He was a talented actor.

3. Which is **not** one of the things that made Jamal feel small inside?
    A. the man at the furniture store
    B. teachers who called attention to him when he made a mistake
    C. having a brother in jail
    D. big kids who laughed at him

4. Who thought up the following plan? Jamal would take over the Scorpions. Then they could make money by carrying for the Spanish guys.
    A. Mack
    B. Indian
    C. Randy
    D. Jamal

Multiple Choice Unit Test 2 *Scorpions*

5. How old is Jamal?
    A. He is fourteen.
    B. He is seventeen.
    C. He is fifteen.
    D. He is twelve.

6. Who said shooting and killing someone ran in the blood?
    A. Randy
    B. Mack
    C. Angel
    D. Jevon

7. True or False: Jamal pulled the gun on Dwayne while they were fighting.
    A. True
    B. False

8. Did Jamal believe he would really throw away the gun?
    A. Yes, he did.
    B. No, he did not.

9. Why did Jamal get fired from his job?
    A. Mr. Gonzalez had heard about the gun.
    B. He was late and was not doing all of his work.
    C. He stole money from the cash register.
    D. Indian and Angel came in and caused trouble.

10. Which event did **not** happened when Jamal and Tito met Indian and Angel in the park?
    A. Jamal told Indian and Angel that Randy said Indian was to be the leader.
    B. Indian told Jamal he was expelled from the Scorpions.
    C. Angel and Indian started beating on Jamal.
    D. Angel pulled out a knife.

Extra Credit: Draw a picture of a scene from the story. Write three or four sentences describing your illustration. Identify the characters, setting, and event that you have drawn.

Multiple Choice Unit Test 2 *Scorpions*

III. Quotations

Directions: Identify the speaker of each quotation. Put the letter of the speaker on the line before the quotation.

A. Indian   B. Jevon   C. Jamal   D. Dwayne   E. Tito

F. Abuela   G. Mama   H. Mr. Davidson   I. Angel   J. Mack

____ 1. "Well, that's better. I know you don't want me to have to take my belt off and straighten you out."

____ 2. "That gun is too much trouble."

____ 3. "I'm not going to give you a warning because I don't think it's going to do any good. So you just go on and do what you want to do. sooner or later you're going to do something that's going to let me put you out of the school. You know that and I know that. Go on now to your classroom."

____ 4. "Pictures! Little boys draw pictures. This is what I want Tito to do. Draw pictures like a little boy."

____ 5. "I was thinking about going to the police and telling them you got a gun."

____ 6. "Your brother's gone, man. You next."

____ 7. "We all born with sense. Lord knows what happens to it along the way."

____ 8. "They layin' low. You waste a couple of guys, and they know you mean what you say."

____ 9. "I'm the leader of the Scorpions."

____ 10. "I see he got the part, but I don't know if he got the heart."

Extra Credit: Draw a picture to go with one of the quotes from the story. Write three or four sentences describing your illustration. Identify the characters, setting, and event that you have drawn.

Multiple Choice Unit Test 2 *Scorpions*

IV. Vocabulary Part 1   Matching

1. parole
2. stocky
3. slick
4. projects
5. bobbing
6. pier
7. glanced
8. vaguely
9. beckoned
10. peer

A. gazed briefly
B. shrewd
C. government funded housing for the poor
D. not clearly expressed
E. a platform over the water
F. made a signaling gesture
G. solidly built; sturdy
H. moving up and down
I. to look or search
J. supervised freedom from prison

Vocabulary Part 2   Directions: Circle the letter next to the word that matches the definition.

11. **an underground, electric railway**
    A. pier
    B. episode
    C. subway
    D. appeal

12. **a small boat used for cruises**
    A. yacht
    B. projects
    C. aroma
    D. squat

13. **rapidly; quickly**
    A. sullenly
    B. hastily
    C. glisten
    D. droopy

14. **bent or sagged downward**
    A. glanced
    B. stammered
    C. clenched
    D. drooped

15. **holding without ownership**
    A. tenements
    B. strut
    C. possession
    D. beckoned

16. **a request for a new court hearing**
    A. parole
    B. appeal
    C. delinquent
    D. juvenile

17. **low and broad**
    A. squat
    B. gravelly
    C. musty
    D. stocky

18. **harmful waste matter**
    A. pollution
    B. compartment
    C. pier
    D. contaminate

19. **run-down apartment buildings**
    A. vials
    B. slits
    C. reflections
    D. tenements

20. **images**
    A. peer
    B. reflections
    C. slits
    D. projects

Name _____ Class _____

ANSWER SHEET   Multiple Choice Unit Tests

I. Matching	II. Mult Choice	III. Quotes	IV Vocab 1	Vocab 2
1. ____	1. ____	1. ____	1. ____	11. ____
2. ____	2. ____	2. ____	2. ____	12. ____
3. ____	3. ____	3. ____	3. ____	13. ____
4. ____	4. ____	4. ____	4. ____	14. ____
5. ____	5. ____	5. ____	5. ____	15. ____
6. ____	6. ____	6. ____	6. ____	16. ____
7. ____	7. ____	7. ____	7. ____	17. ____
8. ____	8. ____	8. ____	8. ____	18. ____
9. ____	9. ____	9. ____	9. ____	19. ____
10. ____	10. ____	10. ____	10. ____	20. ____

ANSWER SHEET KEY   Multiple Choice Unit Test 1 *Scorpions*

#	Matching		Multiple Choice		Quotations		Vocabulary	
	Test 1	Test 2	Test 1	Test 2	Test 1	Test 2	Test 1	Test 2
1	E	G	B	D	C	B	I	J
2	C	I	D	C	I	E	A	G
3	I	D	C	C	J	H	H	B
4	A	H	A	A	H	F	J	C
5	G	F	B	D	D	D	F	H
6	J	A	A	C	F	I	C	E
7	B	E	B	A	E	G	E	A
8	H	J	B	B	B	J	G	D
9	F	C	D	D	G	C	V	F
10	D	B	A	A	A	A	D	I
11							C	C
12							C	A
13							D	B
14							D	D
15							B	C
16							D	B
17							B	A
18							A	A
19							B	D
20							A	B

UNIT RESOURCES

BULLETIN BOARD IDEAS

1. Save one corner of the board for the best of students' *Scorpions* writing assignments. You may want to use background maps of Europe to represent the setting of the novel.

2. Take one of the word search puzzles from the extra activities packet and with a marker copy it over in a large size on the bulletin board. Write the clue words to find to one side. Invite students prior to and after class to find the words and circle them on the bulletin board.

3. Have students find or draw pictures that they think resemble the characters in the book.

4. Invite students to help make an interactive bulletin board quiz. Give each student a half-sheet of paper (about 4"x5') folded in half so that it can open. On the outside flap, have each student write a description of one of the characters in the text. On the inside, they will write the name of the character. You can staple or tack these papers to the bulletin board so that the students can read the descriptions and lift the flaps to find the answers.

5. Collect pictures of Harlem.

6. Make a display of pictures of book jackets and artwork from the various editions of *Scorpions*.

7. Make a "word of the Day" section on the bulletin board. Post one of the vocabulary words, and the context sentence from the book. Under it, put a several blank index cards. Encourage students to write sentences using the word. These can be original or sentences from other books. If the sentence comes from another book, the student should cite the source. You may want to give extra credit to students who complete this activity.

8. Display articles about Walter Dean Myers.

9. Have students design postcards depicting the settings of the book.

10. Display a large map of Harlem and have students find the streets mentioned in the book.

EXTRA ACTIVITIES

One of the difficulties in teaching a novel is that all students don't read at the same speed. One student who likes to read may take the book home and finish it in a day or two. Sometimes a few students finish the in-class assignments early. The problem, then, is finding suitable extra activities for students.

One thing that helps is to keep a little library in the classroom. For this unit on *Scorpions* you might check out from the school or public library other books by Walter Dean Myers. There are also other novels dealing with the problems and challenges of today's youth that students would enjoy reading. Several journals have critiques of the works of Walter Dean Myers. Some of the students may enjoy reading these and responding either in writing or in discussion groups.

Your students who have reading difficulties, or speak English as a second language may benefit from listening to all or part of the book on tape. Or, ask for volunteers to be reading partners and read aloud with the student.

Other things you may keep on hand are word search puzzles. Several puzzles relating directly to *Scorpions* are included in the unit. Feel free to duplicate them.

Some students may like to draw. You might devise a contest or allow some extra-credit grade for students who draw characters or scenes from *Scorpions.* Note, too, that if the students do not want to keep their drawings you may pick up some extra bulletin board materials this way. If you have a contest and you supply the prize. You could, possibly, make the drawing itself a non-refundable entry fee.

Have maps, a globe, and travel brochures on hand for easy reference. Travel agencies and automobile clubs are good sources for these materials.

The pages which follow contain games, puzzles, and worksheets. The keys, when appropriate, immediately follow the puzzle or worksheet. There are two main groups of activities: one group for the unit; that is, generally relating to the *Scorpions* text, and another group of activities related strictly to the *Scorpions* vocabulary.

Directions for the games, puzzles, and worksheets are self-explanatory. The objective here is to provide you with extra materials you may use in any way you choose.

Scorpions Word Search

```
H I C K S P O F F O R D V A F T H M D
M J H A W I P W Q C O G M Z I F I I S
Y T A N T W X Y A O H H H E R C L T C
R C R G F M B T L M T A I L E C J C O
N Y L E N O H B E S H B N A H R V H R
A N E L V O U V A E T U Y Z O R S E P
V C M L L E N R A D N E Z N U C M L I
G D H I N T B L T J E L G O S S W L O
P B C P Z Z G G X E V A W G E R E N N
U F N R O B E R T S E G H N C S I O S
E N E P N N O S Z N S N A F B U L S S
R O E K T W S Z I V R I W R D C L I E
T S R H K O W S V N D S Q A V R I D V
O D G M D R A W I N G Y E N Y A W D E
B I X U I B L D I G E H O D C M J A N
E V B C N T D M I L N V T Y V W T K T
Z A H F B S O B A R E X W G Q Z C Y E
F D B O A T S H U J W N O T N A T S E
F I V E P Q W B T W E L V E M B B M N
```

ABUELA	CATHOLIC	FOURTEEN	MITCHELL	SINGH
ADDISON	CELIA	GONZALEZ	MYRNA	SIXTEEN
ANGEL	DARNELL	GREEN	OSWALDO	SPOFFORD
ASTHMA	DAVIDSON	GUN	PUERTO	STANTON
BASIN	DRAW	HARLEM	RANDY	TITO
BIGGS	DRAWING	HICKS	RICH	TWELVE
BLOOD	DWAYNE	INDIAN	ROBERTS	TWO
BOATS	EIGHT	JEVON	SCORPIONS	WHALEY
BROWN	FIREHOUSE	MACK	SEVENTEEN	WILLIE
BURN	FIVE	MARCUS	SEVENTH	

Scorpions Word Search Answer Key

ABUELA	CATHOLIC	FOURTEEN	MITCHELL	SINGH
ADDISON	CELIA	GONZALEZ	MYRNA	SIXTEEN
ANGEL	DARNELL	GREEN	OSWALDO	SPOFFORD
ASTHMA	DAVIDSON	GUN	PUERTO	STANTON
BASIN	DRAW	HARLEM	RANDY	TITO
BIGGS	DRAWING	HICKS	RICH	TWELVE
BLOOD	DWAYNE	INDIAN	ROBERTS	TWO
BOATS	EIGHT	JEVON	SCORPIONS	WHALEY
BROWN	FIREHOUSE	MACK	SEVENTEEN	WILLIE
BURN	FIVE	MARCUS	SEVENTH	

Scorpions Crossword

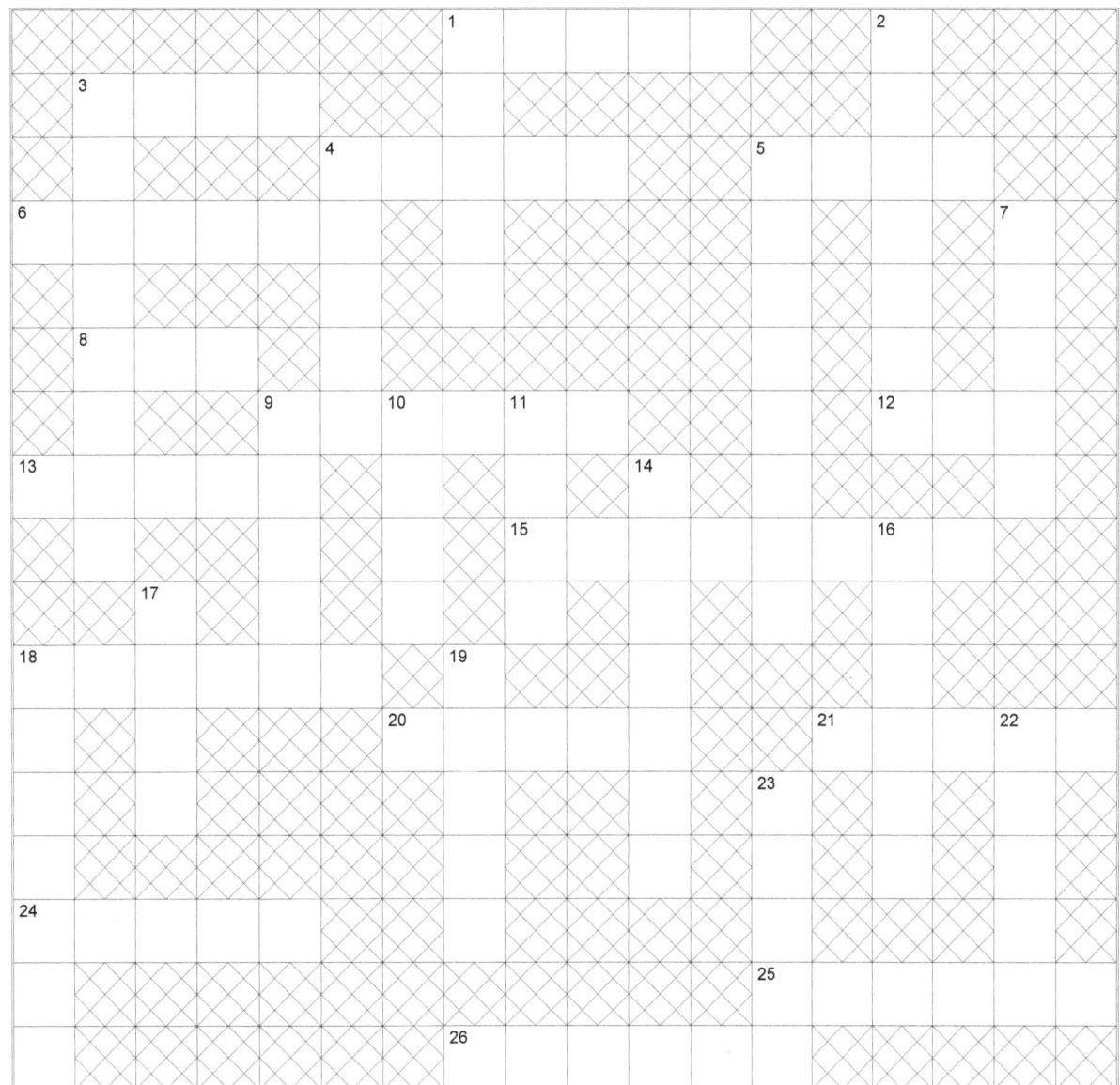

Across
1. Boat ____; Jamal and Tito liked to visit this place
3. At first the lawyer wanted ____ hundred dollars for the appeal
4. First to notice Jamal's gun
5. Jamal liked to ____ and paint
6. ____ Rico; Tito went here after the fight
8. The lawyer wanted ____ thousand dollars for the appeal
9. Tito's ailment
12. What Mack gave Jamal
13. ____ Hicks; told Jamal to act more like a young man
15. Tito's religion
18. Tito's grandmother
20. Sassy's age
21. Reverend ____; prayed with the family
24. Kids were sent to Mr. ____ if they were in trouble
25. Jamal pulled the gun on him during a fight
26. Jerry ____; roughest kid in the school

Down
1. Miss ____; Jamal's favorite teacher
2. Jamal gave one of his to Tito when he left
3. Angel's age
4. Jamal and Tito dreamed of owning them
5. Mr. ____, principal; didn't notice when Jamal was on time
7. Didn't like Dwayne; gave him a disgusted look
9. Said Jamal didn't have any experience
10. ____ Cruz; Jamal's best friend
11. Gave the gun to Jamal
14. Mr. ____ would not loan Mama the money
16. Wondered if Jamal 'had the heard'
17. Mama's ailment
18. Mr. ____ was Randy's lawyer
19. Mrs. ____ wondered what her family was coming to
22. ____ Haven; Randy was in prison there
23. Jamal's older brother who was in jail

Scorpions Crossword Answer Key

							¹B	A	S	I	N		²D		
		³F	I	V	E		R					⁵D	R	A	W
		O			⁴B	L	O	O	D			A			⁷M
⁶P	U	E	R	T	O		W					V			Y
		R			A		N					I			R
		⁸T	W	O		T						I			R
		E			⁹A	S	¹⁰T	H	¹¹M	A		D		¹²G	U	N
¹³J	E	V	O	N		I		A			¹⁴S	S			A
		N		G		¹⁵C	A	T	H	O	L	I	¹⁶C
			¹⁷B	E		O	K	A	N	N
¹⁸A	B	U	E	L	A		¹⁹H		N					D
D		R			²⁰E	I	G	H	T		²¹B	I	G	²²G	S
D		N			C			O		²³R	A		R
I					K			N		A		N	E
²⁴S	I	N	G	H		S			N		E
O									²⁵D	W	A	Y	N	E
N				²⁶W	H	A	L	E	Y

Across
1. Boat ____; Jamal and Tito liked to visit this place
3. At first the lawyer wanted ____ hundred dollars for the appeal
4. First to notice Jamal's gun
5. Jamal liked to ____ and paint
6. ____ Rico; Tito went here after the fight
8. The lawyer wanted ____ thousand dollars for the appeal
9. Tito's ailment
12. What Mack gave Jamal
13. ____ Hicks; told Jamal to act more like a young man
15. Tito's religion
18. Tito's grandmother
20. Sassy's age
21. Reverend ____; prayed with the family
24. Kids were sent to Mr. ____ if they were in trouble
25. Jamal pulled the gun on him during a fight
26. Jerry ____; roughest kid in the school

Down
1. Miss ____; Jamal's favorite teacher
2. Jamal gave one of his to Tito when he left
3. Angel's age
4. Jamal and Tito dreamed of owning them
5. Mr. ____, principal; didn't notice when Jamal was on time
7. Didn't like Dwayne; gave him a disgusted look
9. Said Jamal didn't have any experience
10. ____ Cruz; Jamal's best friend
11. Gave the gun to Jamal
14. Mr. ____ would not loan Mama the money
16. Wondered if Jamal 'had the heard'
17. Mama's ailment
18. Mr. ____ was Randy's lawyer
19. Mrs. ____ wondered what her family was coming to
22. ____ Haven; Randy was in prison there
23. Jamal's older brother who was in jail

MATCHING QUIZ/WORKSHEET 1 - Scorpions

___ 1. ASTHMA   A. Mr. ____ was Randy's lawyer.
___ 2. FIVE   B. Tito's ailment
___ 3. GONZALEZ   C. Mrs. ____ wondered what her family was coming to.
___ 4. BLOOD   D. At first the lawyer wanted ____ hundred dollars for the appeal.
___ 5. SINGH   E. Mrs. ____ told Dwayne to stay after school.
___ 6. ABUELA   F. Miss ____; Jamal's favorite teacher
___ 7. GUN   G. First to notice Jamal's gun
___ 8. FIREHOUSE   H. Jamal and Tito dreamed of owning them.
___ 9. BROWN   I. Randy's age
___10. ADDISON   J. Tito's grandmother
___11. CATHOLIC   K. Scorpion's base was an old one
___12. SCORPIONS   L. ____ Garvey; name of the park
___13. FOURTEEN   M. Wondered if Jamal 'had the heard'
___14. SEVENTH   N. Prison where Mack had been
___15. BOATS   O. The lawyer wanted ____ thousand dollars for the appeal.
___16. HICKS   P. Mrs. Rich said Jamal might spend another year in ____ grade.
___17. MITCHELL   Q. Kids were sent to Mr. ____ if they were in trouble.
___18. WILLIE   R. Last name of boy who raced down the stairs in school with Jamal
___19. ROBERTS   S. Mrs. ____ gave peppermints to students.
___20. MARCUS   T. Tito's religion
___21. SEVENTEEN   U. Angel's age
___22. INDIAN   V. Randy used to be their leader.
___23. TWO   W. What Mack gave Jamal
___24. VELASQUEZ   X. Jamal worked in his bodega.
___25. SPOFFORD   Y. Turned Randy in to a cop a plea.

KEY: MATCHING QUIZ/WORKSHEET 1 - Scorpions

B - 1. ASTHMA   A. Mr. ____ was Randy's lawyer.
D - 2. FIVE   B. Tito's ailment
X - 3. GONZALEZ   C. Mrs. ____ wondered what her family was coming to.
G - 4. BLOOD   D. At first the lawyer wanted ____ hundred dollars for the appeal.
Q - 5. SINGH   E. Mrs. ____ told Dwayne to stay after school.
J - 6. ABUELA   F. Miss ____; Jamal's favorite teacher
W - 7. GUN   G. First to notice Jamal's gun
K - 8. FIREHOUSE   H. Jamal and Tito dreamed of owning them.
F - 9. BROWN   I. Randy's age
A -10. ADDISON   J. Tito's grandmother
T -11. CATHOLIC   K. Scorpion's base was an old one
V -12. SCORPIONS   L. ____ Garvey; name of the park
U -13. FOURTEEN   M. Wondered if Jamal 'had the heard'
P -14. SEVENTH   N. Prison where Mack had been
H -15. BOATS   O. The lawyer wanted ____ thousand dollars for the appeal.
C -16. HICKS   P. Mrs. Rich said Jamal might spend another year in ____ grade.
E -17. MITCHELL   Q. Kids were sent to Mr. ____ if they were in trouble.
Y -18. WILLIE   R. Last name of boy who raced down the stairs in school with Jamal
S -19. ROBERTS   S. Mrs. ____ gave peppermints to students.
L -20. MARCUS   T. Tito's religion
I -21. SEVENTEEN   U. Angel's age
M -22. INDIAN   V. Randy used to be their leader.
O -23. TWO   W. What Mack gave Jamal
R -24. VELASQUEZ   X. Jamal worked in his bodega.
N -25. SPOFFORD   Y. Turned Randy in to a cop a plea.

MATCHING QUIZ/WORKSHEET 2 - Scorpions

___ 1. BLOOD   A. First name of boy who raced down the stairs in school with Jamal
___ 2. DARNELL   B. Randy's age
___ 3. EIGHT   C. ____Hicks; told Jamal to act more like a young man
___ 4. FIREHOUSE   D. Didn't like Dwayne; gave him a disgusted look
___ 5. ANGEL   E. Jamal worked in his bodega.
___ 6. MYRNA   F. Turned Randy in to a cop a plea.
___ 7. SINGH   G. First to notice Jamal's gun
___ 8. DWAYNE   H. Said Jamal didn't have any experience
___ 9. BROWN   I. Boat ____; Jamal and Tito liked to visit this place.
___10. DAVIDSON   J. Setting of the novel
___11. HARLEM   K. ____Garvey; name of the park
___12. JEVON   L. Miss ____; Jamal's favorite teacher
___13. WHALEY   M. At first the lawyer wanted ____hundred dollars for the appeal.
___14. MARCUS   N. Asked Jamal if he had a gun
___15. FOURTEEN   O. Jerry ____; roughest kid in the school
___16. WILLIE   P. Tito's ailment
___17. OSWALDO   Q. Scorpion's base was an old one
___18. BASIN   R. ____ Haven; Randy was in prison there
___19. FIVE   S. Kids were sent to Mr. ____ if they were in trouble.
___20. GREEN   T. Sassy's age
___21. GONZALEZ   U. Jamal pulled the gun on him during a fight.
___22. DRAW   V. Angel's age
___23. RICH   W. Jamal liked to ____ and paint.
___24. ASTHMA   X. Mr. ____, principal; didn't notice when Jamal was on time
___25. SEVENTEEN   Y. Mrs. ____ asked Jamal if he would ever pay attention in class

KEY: MATCHING QUIZ/WORKSHEET 2 - Scorpions

G - 1. BLOOD	A.	First name of boy who raced down the stairs in school with Jamal
N - 2. DARNELL	B.	Randy's age
T - 3. EIGHT	C.	____Hicks; told Jamal to act more like a young man
Q - 4. FIREHOUSE	D.	Didn't like Dwayne; gave him a disgusted look
H - 5. ANGEL	E.	Jamal worked in his bodega.
D - 6. MYRNA	F.	Turned Randy in to a cop a plea.
S - 7. SINGH	G.	First to notice Jamal's gun
U - 8. DWAYNE	H.	Said Jamal didn't have any experience
L - 9. BROWN	I.	Boat ____; Jamal and Tito liked to visit this place.
X -10. DAVIDSON	J.	Setting of the novel
J - 11. HARLEM	K.	____Garvey; name of the park
C -12. JEVON	L.	Miss ____; Jamal's favorite teacher
O -13. WHALEY	M.	At first the lawyer wanted ____hundred dollars for the appeal.
K -14. MARCUS	N.	Asked Jamal if he had a gun
V -15. FOURTEEN	O.	Jerry ____; roughest kid in the school
F -16. WILLIE	P.	Tito's ailment
A -17. OSWALDO	Q.	Scorpion's base was an old one
I - 18. BASIN	R.	____ Haven; Randy was in prison there
M 19. FIVE	S.	Kids were sent to Mr. ____ if they were in trouble.
R -20. GREEN	T.	Sassy's age
E -21. GONZALEZ	U.	Jamal pulled the gun on him during a fight.
W 22. DRAW	V.	Angel's age
Y -23. RICH	W.	Jamal liked to ____ and paint.
P -24. ASTHMA	X.	Mr. ____, principal; didn't notice when Jamal was on time
B -25. SEVENTEEN	Y.	Mrs. ____asked Jamal if he would ever pay attention in class

UNIT WORD SCRAMBLE *Scorpions*

SCRAMBLE	WORD	CLUE
DSANDIO	ADDISON	Randy's lawyer
LANEG	ANGEL	said Jamal didn't have any experience
SAHAMT	ASTHMA	Tito's ailment
LOBDO	BLOOD	first to notice Jamal's gun
OTBSA	BOATS	Jamal and Tito dreamed of owning them
RNOWB	BROWN	Jamal's favorite teacher
UBNR	BURN	Mama's ailment
ECIAL	CELIA	wanted to borrow fifteen cents
NARLDEL	DARNELL	asked Jamal if he had a gun
AVONDIDS	DAVIDSON	principal
GRAINWD	DRAWING	Jamal gave one of his to Tito
WDEANY	DWAYNE	Jamal pulled the gun on him
IGETH	EIGHT	Sassy's age
IREEHUSFO	FIREHOUSE	Scorpion's base was an old one
IEFV	FIVE	the lawyer wanted ___ hundred dollars
EOURENTF	FOURTEEN	Angel's age
AMRLEH	HARLEM	setting of the novel
IKCSH	HICKS	wondered what her family was coming to
NDNIAI	INDIAN	wondered if Jamal "had the heart"
EOVNJ	JEVON	told Jamal to act more like a young man
KACM	MACK	gave the gun to Jamal
LICHMTEL	MITCHELL	told Dwayne to stay after school
YAMNR	MYRNA	didn't like Dwayne
RNYAD	RANDY	Jamal's older brother who was in jail
GSBIG	BIGGS	Reverend ___ prayed with the family
CRIH	RICH	asked Jamal if he would pay attention
OBRETSR	ROBERTS	gave peppermints to students
CROSPIOSN	SCORPIONS	Randy used to be their leader
ESENTVH	SEVENTH	Jamal was in _____ grade
ESITENX	SIXTEEN	Mack's age
NSATNTO	STANTON	would not loan Mama the money
TEVLEW	TWELVE	Jamal's age
ILLEWI	WILLIE	turned Randy in to cop a plea

VOCABULARY RESOURCES

Scorpions Vocabulary Word Search

```
T S B D C E B X R S Y S R Y N G P S J
L V C R L Q L D P T N P M A D L E T U
A E D O S I P E V O S T O C K Y E S V
E N R O M D X I I O L T G H T N R H E
P A D P X P A T E P I L A T E W Q I N
P V W Y T L A B A R C K U M X C F E I
A S K C S S N R C K K S E T M L Q L L
B C D B U U O V T P T N T R I E Q D E
C Q E C S M L G R M T H G R F O R W Y
D O C M A Q M L G S E J A P U Y N E P
E A N X I O U S E M D N R S V T M G D
L B A T J T U A Z N G R T P T W U R V
I E L F A B P F T H L U O R Y Y S A A
N C G N W M M H R B M Y W O G K T V G
Q K L A S L I T S B F J C J P M Y E U
U O Y K W C H N L L I N G E R E D L E
E N P Q D C L E A C L E N C H E D L L
N E K D F V D W Y T S B Z T R J R Y Y
T D V B A N N I S T E R K S L N N N W
```

ACCUSATIONS	DROOPED	PEER	STOOP
ANXIOUS	DROOPY	PIER	STRUT
APPEAL	EPISODE	POLLUTION	STUMBLED
AROMA	GLANCED	PROJECTS	SUBWAY
BANNISTER	GRAVELLY	SHIELD	SULLENLY
BECKONED	HASTY	SLICK	TENEMENTS
CLENCHED	JUVENILE	SLITS	VAGUELY
COMPARTMENT	LINGERED	SQUAT	VIALS
CONTAMINATE	MUSTY	STAMMERED	YACHT
DELINQUENT	PAROLE	STOCKY	

Scorpions Vocabulary Word Search Answer Key

```
              D     E           S     S     Y           P     J
    L         C  L  P  T        N     A           P     E     U
L   A  E  D  O  S  I  P  E  V  O  S  T  O  C  K  Y  E     V
E      E  R  O  M     I  I  O     T  L     H     N  R  S  E
P   P  A     P     P  A  T  E  P  I  L  A  T  E        H  N
P   A     Y     L  A     R  A  R  C     U  M           I  I
A           S  S     R     K  S  E  T  M           E  L  L
         D     U  U  O     T        N  T     I     O  R  E
C        E  C  S  M  L        M  T  H     R     N  D
D   O    C     A  Q     L     S  E     A     U  T     G
E   A  N  X  I  O  U  S  E    D  N        S  T  M  R  D
L   B  A  T        U  A       N  R  T  P     U  R  A  V
I   E  L     A     B     T       L  U  O  R  Y  S  A  G
N   C  G     W  M                M  Y  O        T  V  U
Q   K        A  S  L  I  T  S  B        J  P  Y  E  E  E
U   O  Y              N  L  I  N  G  E  R  E  D  L  L  L
E   N                 E  A  C  L  E  N  C  H  E  D  L  U
N   E              D                       T           Y  Y
T   D     B  A  N  N  I  S  T  E  R        S
```

ACCUSATIONS	DROOPED	PEER	STOOP
ANXIOUS	DROOPY	PIER	STRUT
APPEAL	EPISODE	POLLUTION	STUMBLED
AROMA	GLANCED	PROJECTS	SUBWAY
BANNISTER	GRAVELLY	SHIELD	SULLENLY
BECKONED	HASTY	SLICK	TENEMENTS
CLENCHED	JUVENILE	SLITS	VAGUELY
COMPARTMENT	LINGERED	SQUAT	VIALS
CONTAMINATE	MUSTY	STAMMERED	YACHT
DELINQUENT	PAROLE	STOCKY	

Scorpions Vocabulary Crossword

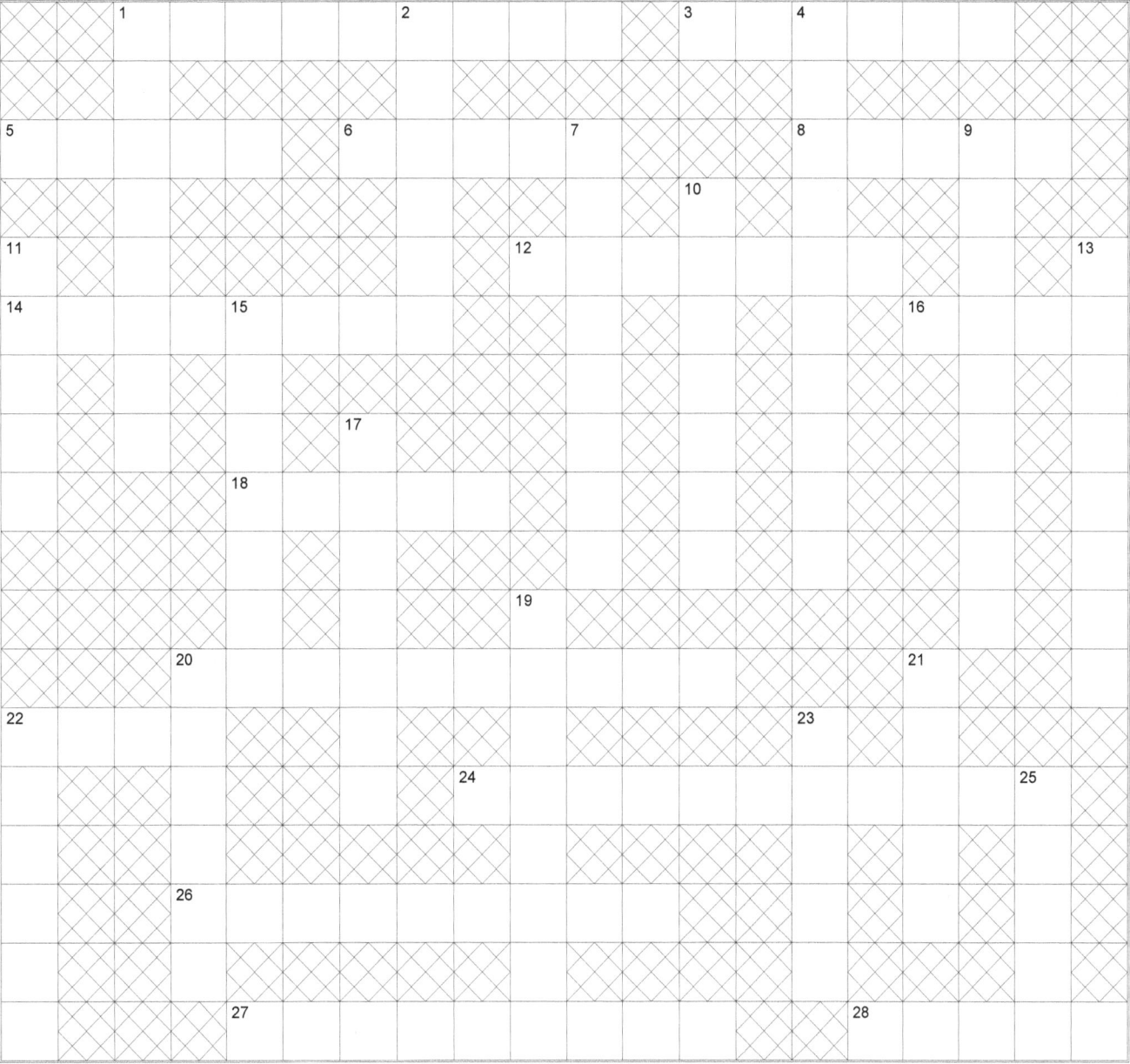

Across
1. A handrail
3. A request for a new court hearing
5. A small boat used for cruises
6. Small containers with stoppers
8. Long, narrow openings
12. Gazed briefly
14. Persisted; stayed
16. To look or search
18. A building's small porch or staircase
20. Someone who disobeys the law
22. A platform over the water
24. Images
26. Harmful waste matter
27. Spoke with involuntary pauses
28. Rapidly; quickly

Down
1. Made a signaling gesture
2. A piece of armor strapped to the arm
4. Holding without ownership
7. With silent resentment
9. Run-down apartment buildings
10. Fearful; panicky
11. Shrewd; tricky
13. Sounding harsh or rasping
15. One part of a serial story or show
17. Moving up and down
19. For or about children or young people
20. Sagging in exhaustion
21. A pleasant odor
22. Supervised freedom from prison
23. A swaggering walk
25. Low and broad

Scorpions Vocabulary Crossword Answer Key

		1 B	A	N	N	2 I	S	T	E	R		3 A	P	4 P	E	A	L	
		E				H								O				
5 Y	A	C	H	T		6 V	I	A	L	7 S		8 S	L	I	T	9 S	
		K						E		U		10 A	S			E	
11 S		O					12 G	L	A	N	C	E	D			N		13 G
14 L	I	N	G	15 E	R	E	D		L		X	S		16 P	E	E	R
I		E		P			L		E		I	S			M		A
C		D		I		17 B			N		O	I			E		V
K			18 S	T	O	O	P		L		U	O			N		E
			O			B			Y		S	N			T		L
			D			B		19 J							S		L
		20 D	E	L	I	N	Q	U	E	N	T		21 A				Y
22 P	I	E	R		N			V				23 S	R				
A		O		24 G		R	E	F	L	E	C	T	I	O	N	25 S	
R		O						N				R			M	Q	
O		26 P	O	L	L	U	T	I	O	N		U			A	U	
L		Y						L				T				A	
E			27 S	T	A	M	M	E	R	E	D		28 H	A	S	T	Y

Across
1. A handrail
3. A request for a new court hearing
5. A small boat used for cruises
6. Small containers with stoppers
8. Long, narrow openings
12. Gazed briefly
14. Persisted; stayed
16. To look or search
18. A building's small porch or staircase
20. Someone who disobeys the law
22. A platform over the water
24. Images
26. Harmful waste matter
27. Spoke with involuntary pauses
28. Rapidly; quickly

Down
1. Made a signaling gesture
2. A piece of armor strapped to the arm
4. Holding without ownership
7. With silent resentment
9. Run-down apartment buildings
10. Fearful; panicky
11. Shrewd; tricky
13. Sounding harsh or rasping
15. One part of a serial story or show
17. Moving up and down
19. For or about children or young people
20. Sagging in exhaustion
21. A pleasant odor
22. Supervised freedom from prison
23. A swaggering walk
25. Low and broad

VOCABULARY MATCHING *Scorpions*

1. appeal
2. clenched
3. glanced
4. musty
5. shield
6. accusations
7. anxious
8. episode
9. stammered
10. vaguely
11. stoop
12. slits
13. bobbing
14. compartment
15. gravelly
16. contaminate
17. stumbled
18. slick
19. strut
20. sullenly

A. gazed briefly
B. spoke with involuntary pauses
C. a small room or section
D. a swaggering walk
E. to make impure
F. a building's small front porch or staircase
G. a piece of armor strapped to the arm
H. tripped
I. stale or moldy
J. fearful; panicky
K. long, narrow openings
L. with silent resentment
M. not clearly expressed
N. a request for a new court hearing
O. charges of wrongdoing
P. sounding harsh or rasping
Q. shrewd; tricky
R. closed tightly
S. one part of a serial story or show
T. moving up and down

ANSWER KEY VOCABULARY MATCHING *Scorpions*

N	1.	appeal	A.	gazed briefly
R	2.	clenched	B.	spoke with involuntary pauses
A	3.	glanced	C.	a small room or section
I	4.	musty	D.	a swaggering walk
G	5.	shield	E.	to make impure
O	6.	accusations	F.	a building's small front porch or staircase
J	7.	anxious	G.	a piece of armor strapped to the arm
S	8.	episode	H.	tripped
B	9.	stammered	I.	stale or moldy
M	10.	vaguely	J.	fearful; panicky
F	11.	stoop	K.	long, narrow openings
K	12.	slits	L.	with silent resentment
T	13.	bobbing	M.	not clearly expressed
C	14.	compartment	N.	a request for a new court hearing
P	15.	gravelly	O.	charges of wrongdoing
E	16.	contaminate	P.	sounding harsh or rasping
H	17.	stumbled	Q.	shrewd; tricky
Q	18.	slick	R.	closed tightly
D	19.	strut	S.	one part of a serial story or show
L	20.	sullenly	T.	moving up and down

VOCABULARY MULTIPLE CHOICE *Scorpions*

1. **an underground, electric railway**
    a. pier
    b. episode
    c. subway
    d. appeal

2. **a pleasant odor**
    a. shield
    b. bannister
    c. musty
    d. aroma

3. **government funded housing for the poor**
    a. delinquent
    b. projects
    c. reflections
    d. squat

4. **bent or sagged downward**
    a. glanced
    b. stammered
    c. clenched
    d. drooped

5. **rapidly; quickly**
    a. sullenly
    b. hastily
    c. glisten
    d. droopy

6. **holding without ownership**
    a. tenements
    b. strut
    c. possession
    d. beckoned

7. **a small boat used for cruises**
    a. yacht
    b. peer
    c. stoop
    d. subway

8. **persisted; stayed**
    a. clenched
    b. glisten
    c. lingered
    d. glanced

9. **supervised freedom from prison**
    a. parole
    b. appeal
    c. delinquent
    d. juvenile

10. **to look or search**
    a. pier
    b. peer
    c. beckoned
    d. stoop

11. **solidly built; sturdy**
    a. squat
    b. gravelly
    c. musty
    d. stocky

12. **small containers with stoppers**
    a. vials
    b. slits
    c. reflections
    d. tenements

13. **harmful waste matter**
    a. pollution
    b. compartment
    c. pier
    d. contaminate

14. **images**
    a. peer
    b. reflections
    c. slits
    d. projects

15. **not clearly expressed**
    a. anxious
    b. hasty
    c. vaguely
    d. sullenly

16. **for or about young people or children**
    a. delinquent
    b. squat
    c. slick
    d. juvenile

ANSWER KEY VOCABULARY MULTIPLE CHOICE *Scorpions*

1. **an underground, electric railway**
   a. pier
   b. episode
   c. **subway**
   d. appeal

2. **a pleasant odor**
   a. shield
   b. bannister
   c. musty
   d. **aroma**

3. **government funded housing for the poor**
   a. delinquent
   b. **projects**
   c. reflections
   d. squat

4. **bent or sagged downward**
   a. glanced
   b. stammered
   c. clenched
   d. **drooped**

5. **rapidly; quickly**
   a. sullenly
   b. **hastily**
   c. glisten
   d. droopy

6. **holding without ownership**
   a. tenements
   b. strut
   c. **possession**
   d. beckoned

7. **a small boat used for cruises**
   a. **yacht**
   b. peer
   c. stoop
   d. subway

8. **persisted; stayed**
   a. clenched
   b. glisten
   c. **lingered**
   d. glanced

9. **supervised freedom from prison**
   a. **parole**
   b. appeal
   c. delinquent
   d. juvenile

10. **to look or search**
    a. pier
    b. **peer**
    c. beckoned
    d. stoop

11. **solidly built; sturdy**
    a. squat
    b. gravelly
    c. musty
    d. **stocky**

12. **small containers with stoppers**
    a. **vials**
    b. slits
    c. reflections
    d. tenements

13. **harmful waste matter**
    a. **pollution**
    b. compartment
    c. pier
    d. contaminate

14. **images**
    a. peer
    b. **reflections**
    c. slits
    d. projects

15. **not clearly expressed**
    a. anxious
    b. hasty
    c. **vaguely**
    d. sullenly

16. **for or about young people or children**
    a. delinquent
    b. squat
    c. slick
    d. **juvenile**

VOCABULARY WORD SCRAMBLE *Scorpions*

SCRAMBLE	WORD	CLUE
UCASATIONCS	ACCUSATIONS	charges of wrongdoing
XINUASO	ANXIOUS	fearful; panicky
PAALEP	APPEAL	a request for a new court hearing
OARMA	AROMA	a pleasant odor
ANISTENRB	BANNISTER	a handrail
EDCBONKE	BECKONED	made a signaling gesture
OBINBGB	BOBBING	moving up and down
DLNCCHEE	CLENCHED	closed tightly
MOCMPARTENT	COMPARTMENT	a small room or section
NANTAOMCITE	CONTAMINATE	to make impure
QLTINEUEDN	DELINQUENT	someone who disobeys the law
RODOPDE	DROOPED	bent or sagged downward
ROYDOP	DROOPY	sagging in exhaustion
SPIEDEO	EPISODE	one part of a serial story or show
LADNGCE	GLANCED	gazed briefly
GINSTEL	GLISTEN	shine
RLAVYGEL	GRAVELLY	sounding harsh or rasping
AYSTH	HASTY	rapidly; quickly
JEENIULV	JUVENILE	for or about children or young people
IGDELNRE	LINGERED	persisted; stayed
YUSTM	MUSTY	stale or moldy
AEROPL	PAROLE	supervised freedom from prison
EREP	PEER	to look or search
IERP	PIER	a platform over the water
ONLUTPILO	POLLUTION	harmful waste matter
OSNSSSIPOE	POSSESSION	holding without ownership
CROJETPS	PROJECTS	government funded housing for the poor
EFSLRETIOCN	REFLECTIONS	images
HIDELS	SHIELD	a piece of armor strapped to the arm
LKISC	SLICK	shrewd; tricky
LISTS	SLITS	long, narrow openings
SUTQA	SQUAT	low and broad
TAMMSEEDR	STAMMERED	spoke with involuntary pauses
TCSYKO	STOCKY	solidly built; sturdy
TOPSO	STOOP	a building's small porch or staircase
TRUST	STRUT	a swaggering walk
BESTMLDU	STUMBLED	tripped
UBAYSW	SUBWAY	an underground, electric railway

ULNLYSEL	SULLENLY	with silent resentment
ENSMETNTE	TENEMENTS	run-down apartment buildings
AEGULYV	VAGUELY	not clearly expressed
ILSVA	VIALS	small containers with stoppers
AHYTC	YACHT	a small boat used for cruises

www.ingramcontent.com/pod-product-compliance
Lightning Source LLC
LaVergne TN
LVHW081537060526
838200LV00048B/2113